240+ Proven Id
Revenues, Profits, ~~~~
Loyalty & Employee Engagement

10x Results

How to Multiply the Value of Your Business

Marc Will
10xResultsPartners.com

10x Results: Multiply the Value of Your Business

Copyright © 2019 Marc Will

All rights reserved. No part of this publication may be reproduced by any mechanical, photographic, phonographic, or electronic process without prior written permission by the author. Neither may it be stored in a retrieval system, transmitted, or otherwise copied for public or private use without this permission. For permission requests, bulk book orders, speaking and consulting inquiries, please contact book@10x-results.com.

This is a work of nonfiction. At the same time, the details of events and names have been changed to protect the author's clients and past employers. Any resemblance is coincidental and not intended.

"10x Results" is an approach, a methodology, to help business owners and CEOs improve the performance of their companies. In this sense, the term 10x Results describes the mindset that characterizes such an endeavor. Under no circumstances should it be seen as a guarantee for results in this or any magnitude—as the realized results depend largely on the company context and the implementation approach that management pursues. In the event you use any of the information in this book, the author assumes no responsibility—financial, legal, or other—for your actions and the resulting consequences.

10x Results is a trademark of Marc Will in the European Union. This also includes the 10x Results approach, the 10x Results pyramid, the 10x Results diagnostic, the 10x Results accelerator, the 10x Results booster, and 10x Results capture. The trademark covers all business sectors, except banking.

Author name	Marc Will
Title	10x Results
Subtitle	240+ Proven Ideas to Boost Revenues, Profits, Customer Loyalty, and Employee Engagement
Subjects	Success in Business, Management, Leadership, Entrepreneurship, Corporate Growth, Corporate Profits, Strategic Planning, Organizational Change, Organizational Effectiveness, Performance, Industrial Management, Creative Ability in Business
Summary	Over the past two decades, the author has helped many of the world's greatest companies achieve their full potential. From small businesses and internet startups to Fortune 500 heavyweights, he has worked hand in hand with entrepreneurs, CEOs, and senior executives to (1) boost revenues, (2) win and keep customers, (3) drive up profits, (4) boost team productivity and motivation, and (5) drive change in the organization. In *10x Results*, he shares with you the secrets that allowed those companies to achieve phenomenal success. *10x Results* is a proven, step-by-step playbook to help bring your business to full potential. It includes 240+ proven ideas to boost revenues, profits, customer loyalty, and employee engagement. The book also contains many practical checklists that you can leverage right away. The principles in this book are based on sound research and the author's two decades of hands-on experience. He was a principal at one of the world's leading strategy consulting firms and sat on the Management Board for Europe at a Fortune Global 100 company—where he was responsible for strategy, customer service, BPO, and transformation.
ISBN	ISBN-13: 978-1727115383

TABLE OF CONTENTS

INTRODUCTION 7

APPETIZER 15
1. The Top 10 for Entrepreneurs and Small Business Owners.... 16
2. The Top 10 for Fortune 500 CEOs 17
3. The Top 10 for Active Investors (Owners, Majority Shareholders, Private Equity and Hedge Funds) 18
4. The Top 10 for Weathering a Recession 19
5. The Top 10 for Maximizing Profits in a Booming Economy .. 20

WHY 10X RESULTS 21
6. What Do I Mean by 10x Results? 22
7. Is 10x Results Realistic? 25
8. Why Many Companies Do Not Achieve Their Full Potential . 30

9. The 10x Results Approach: Realizing the Full Potential of Your Business 34

10. Data Confirms the 10x Results Approach 43

THE FOUNDATION 47

11. Focus, Focus, Focus 48

12. Reduce Complexity and Cut Waste 53

13. Insane Customer Focus 61

14. Getting Better Every Day 65

15. Measure Success 69

16. Bias for Action 73

17. Commit to a Goal and Stick to It When It Gets Tough 76

18. Summary: Key Insights and Action Plan 80

MULTIPLY THE PRODUCTIVITY OF YOUR PEOPLE 83

19. Give Your Team a "Why" That Is Worth Fighting for 84

20. Set the Bar High 88

21. Hire and Keep Only A Players 92

22. Put Your People into Growth Roles 98

23. Delegate Authority and Hold People 100% Accountable 103

24. Make Each Day Count 107

25. Deep Work 113

26. Make Your Meetings and Calls 10x More Effective 117

27. Money Is Not Everything—Publicly Recognize and Praise Excellent Performance 121

28. Manage by Deliverables, Not Tasks 127

29. Keep Your People's Energy Levels High 131

30. Summary: Key Insights and Action Plan 137

DRIVE INNOVATION AND GROWTH 139

31. A Powerful Framework for Business Growth 140

32. The Best Business Growth Engine: Customer Referrals and Testimonials 145

33. Punch above Your Weight: Joint Ventures and Partnerships 149

34. Become World-Class in Winning New Business 153

35. Implement a World-Class Pricing Model 158

36. Take Calculated Risks 164

37. Double Down on Innovation 169

38. Put Your Growth on Steroids: Use Small-Scale Acquisitions to Close Capability Gaps 174

39. Summary: Key Insights and Action Plan 178

REACH PEAK PERFORMANCE 181

40. The 12-Week Year 182

41. Strategy-on-a-Page 186

42. Management Board and Decision Effectiveness 190

43. The Role of Active Investors and Outside Directors 195

44. Build Your Organizational Muscle 198

45. Make Use of New Technology/Digitalization 201

46. Summary: Key Insights and Action Plan 205

Results Capture/ How to Implement 207

47. How to Prioritize/Where to Start 208
48. Effectively Manage Change and Bring in Results 213
49. Your Role as a Business Owner and CEO 218
50. Bringing It All Together—The 10x Results Action Plan 222
51. Next Steps—Where to Take It from Here 229

Acknowledgments 233

About the Author 235

INTRODUCTION

"Ambition is a dream with a V8 engine."
— Elvis Presley

In this book, you will find more than 240 proven ideas to boost your business—grow revenues and profits, increase customer loyalty and employee engagement. Whether you are a Fortune 500 CEO, a small business owner, an active investor, a senior executive, or an internet entrepreneur, this book is written for you. Each of the ideas presented could be worth millions to your business. Some of these ideas you may have already implemented, but I am sure that you will find many more great ideas in this book—ideas that will help you take your business to the next level.

I was very fortunate: I spent the past two decades working with some of the world's greatest companies. We worked on their growth strategies, on their performance improvement programs, on due diligences and post-merger integrations, on large IT transformations, on organizational effectiveness, on corporate and business unit strategy, and many other topics. Over the years, I have seen the power of the 240+ ideas from this book in action. I have seen how they helped both large and small companies achieve exponential growth. Now I want to share these proven ideas with you.

My Story

It was a mild summer morning in 2014. The alarm clock in my hotel room in Basel, Switzerland, was set to 5:30 a.m., but I woke up about an hour earlier. Many thoughts from a meeting that we had the day before kept running through my head.

At that time, I was recently made responsible for the transformation activities in Europe, the Middle East, and Africa at a Fortune Global 100 company. In one of the divisions, we embarked on a large-scale IT, business process, and organizational transformation program. It included offshoring processes to Asia, completely rebuilding the operational IT landscape, and aligning the organizational structures across more than 100 countries.

In the meeting the day before, we realized that we were facing several problems. First, the IT implementation was stalling. With every new country that we approached, the list of "must-have" requirements grew larger and larger. Soon it would be too much to handle. Second, the resistance toward the change was building among employees. Some did not understand why the change was needed. Others believed that it was just too much too fast. We needed to act quickly to ensure that we would get everybody on board again. Last, with several thousand employees involved in the transformation globally, we were starting to lose speed as the program structure became overly bureaucratic. Many people were spending much of their time in meetings and on calls—with little to show for it at the end of the day.

On this summer morning in 2014, I came to the conclusion that I had to write this book. I realized that many companies face similar challenges. And I realized that I could help. My experience from the past two decades—working alongside some of the greatest business leaders on some of their toughest challenges—allowed me to gather valuable strategies and practices to effectively deal with some of the toughest challenges that many business leaders face today.

In this book, you will find the collective insights and best practices of my career thus far. My business career started in the late 1990s when I supported several entrepreneurs and small business owners in restructuring their businesses and returning them to profitability. It continued in the early 2000s by helping a global specialty chemicals company and a multinational bank with their post-merger integrations. A few years later, after I received my MBA, I joined one of the leading and most admired strategy consulting firms in the world. Here, I led large-scale transformation programs and strategy projects for clients in a broad range of industries, like industrial goods and services, oil and gas, transportation, telecommunications, high tech, and consumer goods/retail. Then, I was hired by one of my clients to oversee the transformation activities in Europe, the Middle East, and Africa for one of their divisions. In the Management Board for Europe, I was responsible for transformation, strategy, BPO, and customer service.

I am in a unique position. As a consultant, I have implemented firsthand the growth strategies and performance improvement initiatives that you will read about here. As a senior executive and Board member, I can relate to the challenges that you experience, because I have been in this position myself.

What You Will Get from This Book

This book is not a novel. I do not tell story after story, but instead, I try to give you as many practical ideas as possible—ideas that can be applied right away to drive your business to full potential. In this book you will learn:

- How to **massively increase customer loyalty**, boost revenues by fixing your product and service quality issues, and use effective customer referral and testimonial strategies.
- How to drive the top line with **effective pricing and innovation** strategies.
- How to **attract and retain the best employees.**
- How to **multiply the effectiveness of your people** while keeping them happy and engaged.
- How to effectively **leverage acquisitions, joint ventures (JVs), and partnerships** to boost your business.
- How to **take out complexity and waste** and, in the process, focus your business on the few things that will drive it to **new levels of profitability.**
- … and many more.

My goal when writing this book was to give you an idea book and a practical, no-nonsense workbook to take your business to full potential. I have condensed all insights into roughly 240 pages. Each chapter includes:

- **Checklists** that summarize the most important points. You can use them as a reference list for the points that you need to keep in mind when implementing the ideas in your company.

Introduction

- **10x Results "million $ ideas"**. Those are the most important ideas and insights in each chapter. Out of the 240+ ideas, those are the ones that should definitely trigger epiphanies and aha moments for you. Take these insights and apply them to your business.
- **Moving to action—questions to ask yourself**. Nothing is achieved until action is taken. Therefore, each chapter closes with a few questions for you to ponder. Those questions are designed to start your thinking on how to best implement these insights and ideas in your company.

To give you an appetizer, here is one of the 10x Results "million $ ideas:"

10x Results "Million $ Idea"

One of your most important jobs as a CEO, owner, or manager is to always challenge your team to do things **much** faster, **much** better, **much** cheaper, or sell at a **much** higher price.

Ask: "**What would it take** to produce at half the cost? **What would it take** to get the product to market in half the time? **What would it take** to reduce failure rates by 98 percent? **What would it take** to sell at a 50 percent premium?"

Massively challenging targets get your team to look at non-conventional ways of doing things, and this will ultimately get you massive results. The question "what would it take?" is one of the most powerful

> QUESTIONS. IT GETS YOUR TEAM TO OPEN UP AND DISCUSS NOVEL IDEAS IN A SAFE ENVIRONMENT.
>
> EVEN IF, AT THE END OF THE DISCUSSION, YOU AGREE WITH THE TEAM ON A TARGET THAT IS A BIT BELOW WHAT YOU COMMUNICATED INITIALLY, THE **COMMITTED TARGET WILL STILL BE MUCH, MUCH HIGHER** THAN WHAT EVEN YOU WOULD HAVE IMAGINED BEFORE.

Do not skim the book or glance over the chapters too quickly. I selected each of the points very carefully—they are all worth the attention. It pays to read this book not in one go, but chapter by chapter. After each chapter take time to reflect on the ideas that were presented. Mark important sections, underline, write notes—make this your book. This way you will get the full benefits from this book. When you read the book for the first time, I recommend that you read it in sequence. Later, you can go to the chapter that is most relevant to the problem that you face on that day.

My vision is that you find this book so useful that you decide to carry it around with you every day as a reference book, as an idea book, as a workbook. I will have done a good job if after two years your copy of this book looks very used, or even torn with detailed notes in the margins.

Some of the initiatives in this book may appear to you as very obvious. You may ask yourself: "Aren't we doing this already?" But when you do a reality check of your business with some of your middle managers, you may be surprised at how little of the obvious is actually done today. So, it makes sense to start there. It doesn't need some esoteric new trick. Sometimes just implementing the proven very well will get you a long way.

INTRODUCTION

How This Book Is Structured

The 10x Results approach will be introduced in the next section called *Why 10x Results*. I will explain what exactly I mean when I use the term 10x Results. I will also explain why 10x Results is realistic and achievable. We will jointly look at some of the problems that many companies face when implementing ambitious transformation programs and how the 10x Results approach can help companies address these problems. At the end of this section, we will look at a study that confirms the findings in this book.

The next four sections *(1) Foundation, (2) Multiply the Productivity of Your People, (3) Drive Innovation and Growth, (4) Reach Peak Performance* contain the core ideas of the 10x Results approach. I will highlight many initiatives that you can put in place in your business to drive it to full potential.

The last section *Results Capture/How to Implement* will explore where best to start your journey to full potential. It will give you valuable hints on how to best prioritize and effectively manage the change with your people. It will also explore the critical role that you play in this journey. We will close by putting all ideas into a concrete and tailored action plan for your business.

My Hope

I hope that you will remember this very moment—the moment that you started reading this book—vividly 20 years from now. I hope that this book will have as profound an impact on your life and business as some of the most defining moments in your life (for example when you got promoted to the C-suite or when you decided to start your own business). I understand that this sets the bar for this book very high, but I hope that after reading *10x Results* you can agree with me that this book belongs in this category.

APPETIZER

Before I explain the 10x Results approach and how it will help you realize the full potential of your business, I want to give you a little appetizer on some of the insights that you will find in this book. On the next pages, you will find my "top 10" chapter picks for:

- ✓ Entrepreneurs and small business owners
- ✓ CEOs of Fortune 500 companies
- ✓ Active investors (owners, majority shareholders, private equity, and hedge funds)

I also included a "top 10" list on how to weather a recession and come out of it much stronger, and one on how to maximize profits in a booming economy. Enjoy the read! I hope that this appetizer gets you excited for the main course of this book: The 10x Results approach and a step-by-step guide on how to use it to realize the full potential of your business.

1. THE TOP 10 FOR ENTREPRENEURS AND SMALL BUSINESS OWNERS

One of the key challenges for many entrepreneurs and small business owners is how to ignite strong, sustainable, and profitable business growth. You have a great idea and a good team, but how can this be translated into strong top-line and bottom-line growth? Another challenge is how to professionalize the organization and stabilize business processes without losing flexibility and agility.

My top 10 picks for entrepreneurs and small business owners are the following chapters. I am sure that they will give you a lot of good, practical, and ready-to-implement ideas to address the challenges that you are facing and bring in results quickly.

1. Become World-Class in Winning New Business (chapter 34)
2. The Best Business Growth Engine: Customer Referrals and Testimonials (chapter 32)
3. Give Your Team a "Why" That Is Worth Fighting for (chapter 19)
4. Measure Success (chapter 15)
5. Punch above Your Weight: Joint Ventures and Partnerships (chapter 33)
6. Focus, Focus, Focus (chapter 11)
7. Hire and Keep Only A Players (chapter 21)
8. Implement a World-Class Pricing Model (chapter 35)
9. The 12-Week Year (chapter 40)
10. Make Each Day Count (chapter 24)

2. THE TOP 10 FOR FORTUNE 500 CEOs

One of the key challenges for CEOs of large corporations is how to retain the agility, flexibility, and insane customer focus that many startups and smaller companies still have. So, one of the key priorities is to fight complexity and bureaucracy, and to ensure that there is a clear focus on the three to five key priorities that will drive most of the value for the coming years.

My top 10 picks for CEOs of Fortune 500 companies are the chapters listed below. While I believe that you will profit immensely from all the chapters in this book, I am sure that you will find in the chapters below a lot of novel ideas that will translate to increased profits quickly:

1. Reduce Complexity and Cut Waste (chapter 12)
2. Insane Customer Focus (chapter 13)
3. Focus, Focus, Focus (chapter 11)
4. Effectively Manage Change and Bring in Results (chapter 48)
5. A Powerful Framework for Business Growth (chapter 31)
6. Make Use of New Technology/Digitalization (chapter 45)
7. Give Your Team a "Why" That Is Worth Fighting for (chapter 19)
8. Bias for Action (chapter 16)
9. Your Role as a Business Owner/CEO (chapter 49)
10. Double Down on Innovation (chapter 37)

3. THE TOP 10 FOR ACTIVE INVESTORS (OWNERS, MAJORITY SHAREHOLDERS, PRIVATE EQUITY AND HEDGE FUNDS)

The key challenge for active investors is how to ensure the company's success without being actively involved in the day-to-day management. The way to get there is to hire the best people into managerial roles and to set the bar for success very high. There needs to be an explicit agreement with management on how success will be measured. Then, goal achievement can be monitored, and interventions can be taken, if needed.

My top 10 picks for active investors are in the following chapters. I hope they will give you many useful, novel ideas on how to help bring the company to full potential:

1. The Role of Active Investors and Outside Directors (chapter 43)
2. Set the Bar High (chapter 20)
3. Hire and Keep Only A Players (chapter 21)
4. Measure Success (chapter 15)
5. The 12-Week Year (chapter 40)
6. A Powerful Framework for Business Growth (chapter 31)
7. Delegate Authority and Hold People 100% Accountable (chapter 23)
8. Put Your Growth on Steroids: Use Small-Scale Acquisitions to Close Capability Gaps (chapter 38)
9. Your Role as a Business Owner/CEO (chapter 49)
10. Take Calculated Risks (chapter 36)

4. THE TOP 10 FOR WEATHERING A RECESSION

The key to weathering a recession successfully and coming out much stronger is to start preparing one or two years before the recession hits. Fortunately, there are sound macroeconomic indicators that can help you predict when a recession will hit (e.g., yield curve, GDP decline, stock market bubbles and P/E ratios, years since last recession).

The best time to get great talent from the market or to acquire great companies is during a recession; the multiples will be much lower than during the boom years. But you need to have the cash for it, and this is what the one to two years before the recession are for.

Below are my top 10 chapter picks on how to weather a recession. Enjoy the read and learn from the ideas so that when the next recession hits, you can profit from it.

1. Measure Success (chapter 15)
2. Insane Customer Focus (chapter 13)
3. Focus, Focus, Focus (chapter 11)
4. Reduce Complexity and Cut Waste (chapter 12)
5. Punch above Your Weight: JVs/Partnerships (chapter 33)
6. Your Role as a Business Owner/CEO (chapter 49)
7. Hire and Keep Only A Players (chapter 21)
8. The 12-Week Year (chapter 40)
9. Delegate Authority and Hold People 100% Accountable (chapter 23)
10. Put Your Growth on Steroids: Use Small-Scale Acquisitions to Close Capability Gaps (chapter 38)

5. The Top 10 for Maximizing Profits in a Booming Economy

Companies typically leapfrog their competitors during a recession. It is much harder to outpace the competition during a boom period when everybody is making a solid profit.

Leading companies need to optimize all levers to drive strong business growth: prospecting and closing, pricing, innovation, acquisitions and partnerships, insane customer focus, and strong financial management.

Below you can find my top 10 picks on how to get max profits from a booming economy. Enjoy the read. I am sure that you will find many valuable ideas to further drive your business growth.

1. A Powerful Framework for Business Growth (chapter 31)
2. Become World-Class in Winning New Business (chapter 34)
3. Set the Bar High (chapter 20)
4. Take Calculated Risks (chapter 36)
5. Double Down on Innovation (chapter 37)
6. Implement a World-Class Pricing Model (chapter 35)
7. Insane Customer Focus (chapter 13)
8. Punch above Your Weight: JVs/Partnerships (chapter 33)
9. The 12-Week Year (chapter 40)
10. Keep Your People's Energy Levels High (chapter 29)

WHY 10X RESULTS

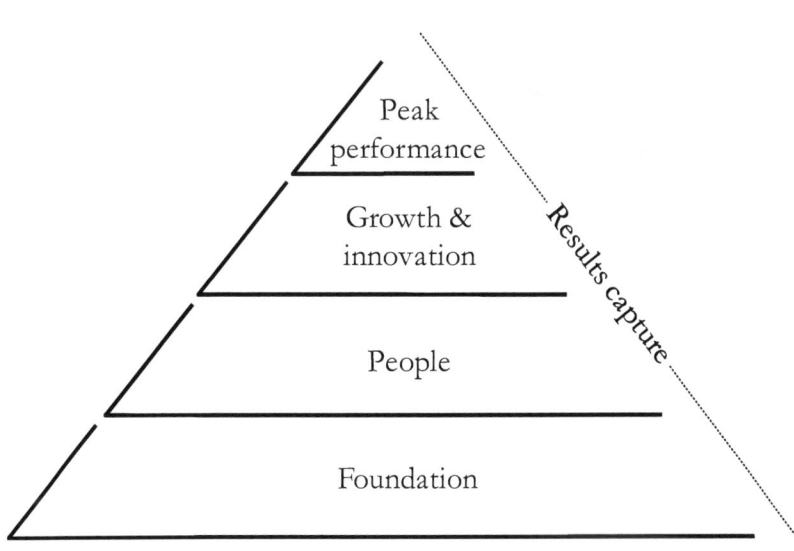

6. WHAT DO I MEAN BY 10X RESULTS?

"Fit no stereotypes. Don't chase the latest management fads. The situation dictates which approach best accomplishes the team's mission."

— Colin Powell

10X RESULTS "MILLION $ IDEA"

I DEFINE **"10X RESULTS"** AS THE AMBITION TO INCREASE THE MARKET VALUE OF YOUR BUSINESS BY A FACTOR OF 10 WITHIN THE NEXT FIVE YEARS.

AS AN EXAMPLE, FOR A PUBLICLY TRADED COMPANY WITH A MARKET CAP OF $1 BILLION TODAY, THE AMBITION WOULD BE TO BRING IT TO $10 BILLION WITHIN THE NEXT FIVE YEARS.

When my clients hear the definition of 10x Results for the first time, they typically ask me two questions: (1) Why 10x—wouldn't 2x or 5x be more realistic? (2) Why five years? Let me address these questions right away.

Why 10x? Wouldn't 2x or 5x be more realistic? 10x stands for an ambition level. You need to work on all areas of your business and bring your company to full potential to get in the range of 10x. This is an extremely ambitious goal—a goal that will stretch you. And it will stretch your organization to become as great as it can be. It inspires unorthodox thinking and the questioning of long-held beliefs.

It inspires you and your team to get up in the morning energized, and when the results start rolling in, your team will want to aim even higher. It mandates that you deliver excellent service to your customer. It mandates that you look at all ways to grow your business and make it more effective. It inspires the best in you and your team.

Having said this, 10x is not an absolute number. It means aiming for the best that your company can be. If you are already the leader in your industry and you have continuously outgrown your peers by a large margin over the past couple of years, then maybe 5x or even 2x is the right ambition level for your business. Or if you have had a few bad years and lost significant ground to the competition, then maybe 20x or even 30x is the better ambition level. What this means is:

10X RESULTS "MILLION $ IDEA"

THE GOAL IS TO **GET YOUR BUSINESS TO FULL POTENTIAL OVER THE NEXT FIVE YEARS. TO MAKE IT THE BEST THAT IT CAN BE:**

(1) WITH VERY LOYAL CUSTOMERS WHO CONTINUOUSLY REFER YOU TO THEIR FRIENDS AND BUSINESS ASSOCIATES;

(2) WITH MOTIVATED, ENGAGED, AND HIGHLY PRODUCTIVE EMPLOYEES;

(3) WITH BUSINESS GROWTH AND AN INNOVATION ENGINE THAT LEAVES COMPETITORS IN THE DUST;

(4) WITH UNPARALLELED PROFIT GROWTH FOR YOU AND YOUR SHAREHOLDERS.

Why five years? The average tenure of a CEO is five years. This is also the right amount of time to not only realize quick win gains, but to also address the important structural topics of your business and bring it to full potential. It allows you to look at all aspects of your business and make sure that it is the best that it can be.

Also here, there may be companies—especially smaller startups or entrepreneur-led, medium-sized businesses—that can go through this full potential process in three years or just one year. At the same time, for some Fortune 500 companies, the process may even take a bit longer than five years. And that is okay. What I am saying is that you should aim to get your company to full potential in a realistic timeline. And for most companies, this will be around five years.

7. Is 10x Results Realistic?

> *"We choose to go to the Moon in this decade and do the other things, not because they are easy, but because they are hard; because that goal will serve to organize and measure the best of our energies and skills, because that challenge is one that we are willing to accept, one we are unwilling to postpone, and one we intend to win."*
>
> — John F. Kennedy

On average, publicly traded companies are able to grow their market value between 5 and 15 percent each year. After five years, this leads to a cumulative increase in company value somewhere between 30 and 100 percent.

With 10x Results, we aim to increase the value of your business by a factor of 10. Does this mean that the 10x Results ambition level is unrealistically high? Let's look at the underlying value drivers in more detail to answer this question:

10x Results "Million $ Idea"

What does it mean to **10x the value of your business** over the next five years? What would you have to achieve to make this happen?

It means, for example, **growing your revenues by an additional 10 percent each year** over the next five years, and at the same time **increasing your profit margin by 2 percentage points a year.** Over five years, this would

---

10x Results: Multiply the Value of Your Business

> ADD UP TO A 10 PERCENTAGE POINT INCREASE IN YOUR PROFIT MARGIN—SO, FOR EXAMPLE, FROM 5 PERCENT TO 15 PERCENT.
>
> ADMITTEDLY, THIS IS A VERY AMBITIOUS GOAL FOR MANY COMPANIES. BUT AT THE SAME TIME, IT IS **A GOAL THAT IS ACHIEVABLE FOR MANY IF YOU ARE ABLE TO BRING YOUR BUSINESS TO FULL POTENTIAL.**

How did I arrive at these numbers? The market value of a company is, in simple terms, dependent on two factors: (1) the profits that the business generates and (2) the profit growth trajectory. The second factor is also why some tech or internet businesses can be valued at such a high price. Their current profits may be low, but the expected business and profit growth is very high.

Let's take a look at an example to illustrate: A company has revenues of $2 billion. At a 5 percent profit margin, it generates $100 million in profits. Historically, the company was able to grow revenues by 5 percent a year; the profit margin remained flat at 5 percent. If the company continued on this path, it would drive up revenues to $2.55 billion and profits to $128 million after five years.

If we now assume that the company can grow revenues at a higher rate—15 percent instead of 5 percent per year—the total revenues after five years would have grown to $4 billion. Under the assumption that the company can increase its profit margin over these five years from 5 percent to 15 percent, this would translate into profits of $600 million in the fifth year. This alone is already 6x-ing the profits of the company from $100 million to $600 million.

But now comes the kicker. Due to the significant increase in profitability growth over these five years, the expected future growth trajectory for the company changes, which leads to an increase in the valuation multiple for the company. You can think of this as the P/E multiple. Taking the 6x in profits together with the increase in the valuation multiple will get you into the range of 10x Results.

Now that we have established that 10x Results is achievable under the assumptions of 10 percent additional revenue growth per year and a 2 percentage point increase in your profit margin per year, let's look at what measures you can put in place to drive up revenues and profitability:

CHECKLIST: IMPORTANT LEVERS TO GROW REVENUES BY AN ADDITIONAL 10 PERCENT A YEAR

- ✓ **Drive up customer loyalty:** Customer loyalty is the holy grail of revenue growth initiatives. More loyal customers will lead to less churn and more repeat purchases at lower selling costs and typically a greater share of wallet. Promoters (very loyal customers) will refer you to their friends and business associates, which will again drive up your revenues.
- ✓ **Optimized pricing:** This is one of the most important revenue and especially profitability levers, yet many companies undermanage their pricing. They do not adjust prices regularly based on changing market conditions. They do not review and adjust their pricing model; this is money left on the table.
- ✓ **Fire up your innovation engine:** Over time, the profitability on any given product or service declines (mainly as a result of increased competition from other companies that also want to have a piece of the profits). So, innovation is vital to keep profitability levels high or even increase them. The innovation spectrum is broader than most people might initially think: product innovation, service innovation, marketing innovation, service delivery innovation, pricing innovation, and so on.
- ✓ **Acquisitions/joint ventures/partnerships:** If done right, acquisitions, JVs, and partnerships are perfect ways to close capability gaps quickly and build a product and solution portfolio that competitors cannot match. This, in turn, leads to higher revenues and profits.

So, the question for you is: Looking at these levers, do you believe that you can grow revenues by an additional 10 percent a year? If you apply them to full potential? Many people would answer yes. I hope you can too. Great. Then, let's look at the profitability side:

CHECKLIST: IMPORTANT LEVERS TO INCREASE YOUR PROFIT MARGIN BY 2 PERCENTAGE POINTS A YEAR

- ✓ **Focus and cut complexity/waste:** Over time, waste and complexity creep into all businesses. This can be things like manual reports for select customers that you agreed to five years ago that are not needed anymore, but you do them anyway out of habit. Or it could be legacy product lines that have made a loss for the last couple of years, but you did not close them because you had other things to focus on. It makes sense to review your business practices every three to five years through this lens: "Does it make sense to invest valuable resources on this activity when those resources could be deployed elsewhere at a much higher benefit to the company?" This can also include offshoring and outsourcing certain activities that can be done more effectively or cheaper at other locations or by other companies.
- ✓ **Streamline business processes:** Complex business processes that cut through many departments with 10 or more approval steps and little automation, plus extra process steps for special customers—this is the reality in many companies. Optimize your business processes through these lenses: How can we increase (1) process speed, (2) process quality, (3) process automation, and decrease (4) process and approval steps?
- ✓ **Increase your people effectiveness:** Do your people work on the most important topics for the company? Do they have specific, ambitious, individual targets that will allow them to

do their greatest work? Are your meetings and calls as effective as they can be? Does everybody take ownership and fix customer issues the first time they occur?

Also here, the question for you is: Looking at these levers, do you believe that you can increase the profit margin in your business by 2 percentage points each year? If you apply the levers to full potential? I hope that you can answer "ambitious, but possible."

8. Why Many Companies Do Not Achieve Their Full Potential

"Success is not final, failure is not fatal; it is the courage to continue that counts."
— Winston Churchill

Bill is the CEO of a multinational technology company that I worked with a few years back. At that time, the company had been through almost 10 years of declining revenues and profits. Here is what happened: The company resulted from a merger of two formerly very successful companies—one headquartered in the U.S., the other in Europe. Both faced challenges from accelerating technology cycles and stiff competition from low-cost Asian competitors. So, they decided to merge. After the merger announcement, they spent more than three years integrating the two companies. Time and again they hit roadblocks. At one time, it was the IT systems that proved too difficult to integrate. Another time, it was the strict labor regulations in Europe including frequent production delays due to strikes. Over these three years, the company was almost entirely internally focused and continuously lost ground versus more aggressive competitors. Then, the 2008 global financial crisis hit. The company initiated another massive cost-cutting program. As a result, the innovation pipeline was killed, and the best people left the company for the competition.

Do some of these challenges sound familiar to you? If they do, you are not alone. A number of my past clients experienced the same challenges. The problem with this is that those challenges prohibit many companies from achieving their full potential.

Before I describe the approach on how to best fix this in the next chapter, I want to quickly highlight some of the most prevailing problems that I saw.

Stop and go: Some companies constantly operate in stop and go mode. Either they are fully on the brakes with massive cost-cutting, or they push the accelerator to its limit by announcing large-scale acquisitions. This approach prohibits them from reaching their full potential. In periods of massive cost-cutting, the best people start to leave and many growth initiatives and innovations that were carefully planned and nurtured die. Yes, the cost-cutting measures help the company in the short term. But at the same time, they also amputate the company's ability to grow going forward. With growth initiatives and innovations killed—and the best people gone—those companies spend the first one to two years after a recession just rebuilding what they have unnecessarily destroyed.

Actually, the best time to plant the seeds for growth is during a recession. You can buy great businesses with complementary capabilities at a discount. You can hire great talent who would otherwise never leave their current employer. But instead, many companies do exactly the opposite. They pursue acquisitions during boom times when the best acquisition targets come at a massive premium, which makes it very hard to reap any net benefits from that acquisition. Even more, to recoup at least part of the high acquisition price, they have to initiate a brutal cost-cutting or synergy capture program.

Measures do not address the root causes: Some companies realize that they have not been able to grow the business over the last couple of quarters, so they try to fix the issue by paying top dollar to buy another company. Soon, they realize that while revenues are now at a higher level, profits are not. Actually, it's quite the contrary; as a result of the high acquisition costs and costly integration efforts, profits are significantly down. The problem is that the root causes for the missing business growth are in other areas: (1) no structured investments in innovations/dry innovation pipeline, (2) ineffective sales and marketing that is not in sync with what the customers' most burning issues are, (3) no pricing strategy—at least the pricing strategy has not been reviewed and optimized for the last couple of years.

Also, on the cost side, many companies operate at the surface level and not on the root causes. Companies implement an across-the-board 10 percent budget cut. Or they implement an across-the-board 5 percent headcount reduction. Still, the root causes lie deeper: (1) business complexity and waste, (2) unclear focus on what really drives value, (3) employees exhausted and not held accountable, (4) lost focus on customer. Only when these issues are fixed, can any company expect sustainable improvements in their profitability levels.

Using only half of the strategy toolkit: Many companies have five to maybe seven distinct strategies that they use. When profit margins go down, they cut personnel costs and discretionary expenditures. When cash goes down, they play with their working capital and sometimes sell and lease back assets. When revenues go down, they play with pricing and sometimes stuff the channels. While all of these strategies have their place, it is like driving a Ferrari in second gear—the machine has so much more to offer—leverage it.

The reality is that the strategies that I just mentioned are all but a small fraction of what can be done. And more often than not there are additional strategies that can and should be employed: How about partnership agreements to access new customer segments and sales channels instead of acquisitions? How about barter trade deals during a recession with strategic partners, where both get what they need at a significant discount. How about making acquisitions during a downturn when the acquisition multiples/the price you pay is sometimes only half of what you would pay during booms. Smart strategy means looking at the entire toolkit and selecting the best tool for the job.

Loss of customer focus: Some companies are so focused on their internal transformation agendas that they start losing sight of the customer. The danger here is that this often becomes visible only when it is too late. You will still see growth in customer numbers and revenue, but just not as much as it could be.

Only partial view of what is possible: Here are a few questions that only a select few companies have asked themselves: What is our customer full potential? How can we achieve it? What is our people full potential? How can we achieve it? What is our growth full potential? How can we achieve it? Not asking the right questions means that they have only a partial view of what is possible. This means that they will not be able to bring their entire business to full potential.

Low ambition level: Some companies—when setting their profit targets for the next year—use the "current year plus x percent method." Who said that 5 percent or 8 percent is the right number? Maybe when looking at the right levers and optimizing them a 20 percent increase would be more adequate. Or even 50 percent and more. Many companies stifle their growth by adjusting their ambition level to "what is normal" in their industry or business. But with this mindset, those companies will never realize extraordinary results.

10X RESULTS "MILLION $ IDEA"

TO BRING YOUR COMPANY TO FULL POTENTIAL—TO MAKE IT THE BEST IT CAN BE—IT IS **ESSENTIAL THAT YOU QUESTION SOME OF THE APPROACHES THAT YOU USED IN THE PAST.**

THIS BOOK WILL HELP YOU TO DO JUST THAT. IT WILL ALSO GIVE YOU THE **IDEAS, TOOLS, AND CHECKLISTS TO REIGNITE STRONG, PROFITABLE GROWTH.**

9. The 10x Results Approach: Realizing the Full Potential of Your Business

> *"Follow effective action with quiet reflection. From the quiet reflection will come even more effective action."*
> — Peter Drucker

Over the past two decades, I got to work with some of the world's greatest companies in more than 30 different industries. From Fortune 500 heavyweights to internet startups. We worked on growth initiatives, performance improvement programs, due diligences, post-merger integrations, IT transformations, organizational effectiveness, corporate and business unit strategy, and turnarounds.

The 10x Results approach contains the best of the best insights from working with these great companies. It helps you avoid the pitfalls that I described in the previous chapter. It works for small and large companies from all walks of life. In this sense, the 10x Results approach is like the numbers in a combination lock—when you look at all profit levers and set them to full potential, the lock opens, and you can enjoy the sight of seeing your business operate at its best.

The 10x Results Pyramid

Building a strong business is like building a pyramid that can endure millennia. First, you need a strong foundation. Then, you can build layer after layer of excellence on top of each other. The 10x Results approach follows the same principles; therefore, I have chosen to illustrate the approach using a pyramid. Overall, the 10x Results approach includes 35 levers, or initiatives, that you can pull from to realize the full potential of your business. These 35 individual levers fall into five major categories, or as I call them, layers of the pyramid: (1) *Foundation*, (2) *People*, (3) *Growth and Innovation*, (4) *Peak performance*, and (5) *Results capture*. The following graphic illustrates this integrated approach:

10X RESULTS APPROACH: THE 10X RESULTS PYRAMID ADDRESSES ALL ASPECTS OF BUSINESS FULL POTENTIAL

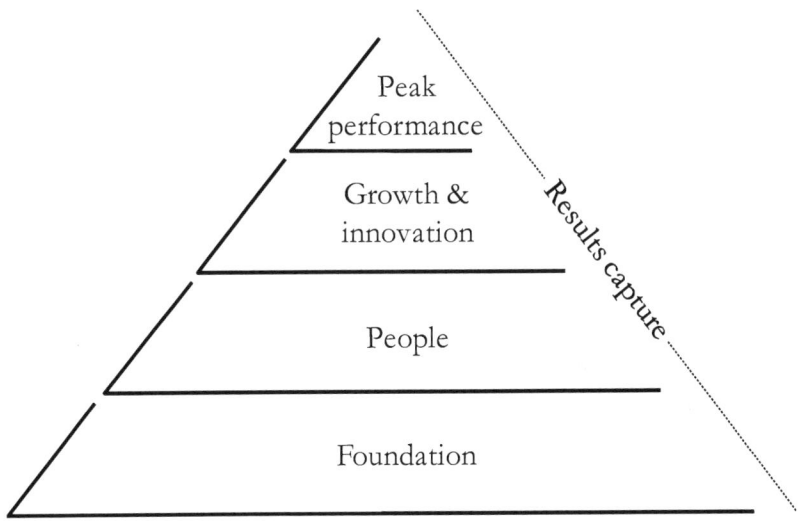

As you can see, *Results capture* integrates the layers of the pyramid. It acts as the glue between the initiatives; it allows you to manage the change effectively and bring in the results quickly.

I will now highlight the main elements of each layer of the 10x Results pyramid. Each of these layers will be covered in detail in the following chapters of the book.

Foundation: As mentioned before, a strong foundation will give your business stability. It will allow you to effectively build other initiatives on top. It starts with *taking out the complexity and waste* that has crept into your business over the years. Many of the problems that companies face—quality issues, process breakdowns, spiraling costs—have their origin here. Addressing this root cause will help you get these problems under control.

Another key lever is *focus*. One of the main reasons why many companies are not able to grow revenues and profits consistently at a high rate is this lack of focus: Trying to serve too many customer segments, trying to offer too many products and services, trying to drive too many initiatives. As a result, those companies spread their resources too thin and become merely average in many areas. But average will not allow you to grow your business. Focus will allow you to become world-class in your chosen field, and this will enable you to drive revenues and boost profit margins.

Also, I will talk about ensuring *insane customer focus* and the massive benefits that this focus brings. Many companies, especially large corporations, are sometimes focused too much on internal issues, and in the process, lose sight of their customers.

Four more principles are part of the foundational layer of the pyramid: (1) In *getting better every day* I argue that successful improvement and change is not something that happens in huge steps, but rather in small, incremental steps, day by day. If you keep continually improving from one day to the next, you will realize that when the year comes to a close, you will have made massive progress. Progress that you could have never achieved in one big step. (2) *Measure success* will show you that by defining the right, few, leading key performance indicators (KPIs) and managing your business along them will allow you to take a giant leap forward across all dimensions. (3) *Ensuring a bias for action* argues that there is a time to think and a time to act. Unfortunately, many companies overthink and act too little too late. Correcting this, testing ideas, and running small-scale pilots will ignite growth in your business. Last but not least, in (4) *commit to a goal and stick to it*, I argue that it is important that once the right decision is made, to also see it through. Many great companies have lost their way because they stepped back from an initiative at the first sign of resistance. It is normal that people are resistant to change. There are effective ways to manage this change.

People: Once, you have built a strong foundation, you can turn to realizing your people full potential. In many companies—large and small—employees are working at, maybe, a 40 to 60 percent effectiveness level. They spend countless hours in unproductive meetings and calls, do not take full ownership, and often do not deliver to full expectations. In some cases, the reason is also that their managers are not able to communicate expectations effectively. Many employees exhibit little passion for the job, feel exhausted, and ultimately deliver shallow work or no meaningful output at all. They are not incentivized and motivated effectively. The people initiatives will address all of these topics. They will allow you to bring your people to full potential, while at the same time boosting their morale, engagement, and keeping their working hours stable or even reducing them.

Growth and Innovation: With a strong foundation and people who operate at full potential, you can build your growth and innovation engine. It starts by understanding what really drives growth and what role customer referrals and testimonials can play in driving growth. Then, I discuss how to punch above your weight by using JVs and partnerships, and how to increase your hit rate in winning new business. I talk about pricing as one of the most effective, and yet underleveraged, ways to drive both revenues and profits. The section closes with improving your risk-taking, igniting your innovation engine, and building your capabilities effectively through small-scale, focused acquisitions.

Peak performance: Peak performance is the top layer of the pyramid. It builds on the other three layers and allows you to even further accelerate your profitable growth. We will explore effective strategy setting and communications, Board and decision effectiveness, and outpacing the competition by implementing a "12-week year." I will also show you ways to effectively build your organizational muscle and make the best use of new technologies and digitalization. Some of the recommendations may surprise you.

Results capture: As mentioned before, results capture acts as the glue between the other four layers. It ensures that you address your transformation in a smart and prioritized way. It also shows you how to effectively manage change and get buy-in from your employees. It shows you the role that you need to play in this transformation, and it will also allow you to develop your own, targeted 10x Results implementation plan. Finally, I will talk about additional ways to get max results as quickly as possible.

The sequence of these steps and the depiction in the 10x Results pyramid are not accidental. The foundational elements are the basis for everything that comes on top of it. Taking out complexity, focusing on what is important, and insane customer focus, for example, are what will allow you to multiply the performance of your people and drive innovation and growth. After you have reached full potential in all these areas, you implement the peak performance measures, which can allow you to surpass even your strongest competitors. All elements are integrated from day one using the results capture toolkit to ensure that change is managed carefully and results are brought in quickly.

The Underlying Principles for 10x Results

The 10x Results approach is based on 10 principles. These 10 principles are the backbone for all the initiatives that are presented in this book. They are what will allow you to realize exceptional profitable growth.

10x Results "Million $ Idea"

The 10x Results approach is guided by 10 principles that, if applied consistently, will put your company on a new growth trajectory:

(1) Focus: Don't try to do it all and become mediocre in the process. Focus on selected customer segments, selected products/services and become world class in what you do. Only then will you be able to attract and keep loyal customers.

(2) Simplify and cut complexity: Complex processes, complex and long decision-making processes, complex products and services is what can derail you. Fight complexity. Make simplicity in everything you do one of your company's mottos.

(3) Insane customer focus: Who pays your bills? Who does your company exist for? Yes, your customers. Keep this front and center for everybody in the company, not just the sales and customer service teams.

(4) Constant, small improvements/getting better every day: Big change efforts often fail. It is the small, daily improvements—compounded over months and years—that will make a big difference. Instill a mindset of "better every day."

(5) Bias for action and smart risk-taking: Inaction is the enemy of greatness. If you believe that an idea is great, then run a small pilot. You will learn a lot from it; many great companies were born from this mindset. Understand the risk profile, and hedge the downside.

(6) MEASURE SUCCESS: Understand the key lead indicators for success in your business. It is typically less than 10—sometimes even only five. Having focus on the five to 10 lead KPIs that drive real value in your business will give you clarity in managing the company and decision making.

(7) HIRE AND KEEP ONLY A PLAYERS: Passion and attitude are often more important than an Ivy League MBA. Passion for the job and for your company's mission is more important than the best technical skill. Technical skill can be taught, but you cannot teach passion and attitude. Keeping C players—or even B players—in your company will demotivate your A players, and in the process, you will lose them. Only A players attract A players.

(8) UNLEASH YOUR PEOPLE: Give them a "why" that is worth fighting for, and set the expectations for their performance very high. Delegate authority to them and hold them 100 percent accountable. Praise them for every good performance and reprimand them for everything that was sub-par. This will help them grow; before long you will be surprised at what they are capable of.

(9) RELEASE THE BRAKES ON REVENUE GROWTH: Pricing full potential. Effective referral and testimonial systems to multiply your success in new customer acquisition. Joint ventures and partnerships. Smart capability-based acquisitions. Focused innovation in areas that allow you to differentiate. Once you start looking into all these areas, you will realize that you can double, quadruple, or even 10x your top-line growth.

> **(10) MANAGE THE CHANGE FROM DAY ONE/CO-CREATE WITH YOUR PEOPLE:** EFFECTIVELY MANAGING THE CHANGE BEFORE RESISTANCE SURFACES IS A CORNERSTONE OF GREAT COMPANIES. INVOLVING YOUR LEADERSHIP TEAM AND ALSO KEY MULTIPLIERS AMONG YOUR EMPLOYEES EARLY IN THE PROCESS WILL HELP YOU ACHIEVE THIS. TRUST IS THE FOUNDATION FOR CHANGE MANAGEMENT SUCCESS.

Principles one through six, you will see explained in more detail in the *Foundation* section of this book. Principles seven and eight are in the *People* section. And principles nine and 10 are in the *Innovation and Growth* and *Peak Performance* sections, respectively.

I want to close this chapter with a quick review of how the 10x Results approach helps you address the shortcomings of the historical management approaches that we discussed in the previous chapter:

FACT BOX: HOW 10X RESULTS ADDRESSES THE SHORTCOMINGS OF TRADITIONAL APPROACHES

- ✓ **Addresses the root causes:** The 10x Results approach addresses the problems at the root and not at a superficial level. For example, the "people" initiatives will allow you to create a high-performance organization composed of A players who are freed from their shackles and ready to take on any challenge.
- ✓ **Integrated approach:** The 10x Results approach is not a loose combination of individual best practices. Instead, each initiative will complement and amplify the impact of the other initiatives.
- ✓ **Flexible:** 10x Results is not a one-size-fits-all approach. It al-

lows you to customize the individual elements to the specific needs of your business—whether it is a small or large enterprise, or during a boom or bust period. The 10x Results approach is flexible enough to accommodate for these factors and still be effective.

- ✓ **The right sequence:** First, you need to get your house in order, before you can pursue other growth opportunities. The two base layers of the pyramid—"foundation" and "people"—will help you do just that.
- ✓ **Focus on results capture from day one:** Change management starts well before the change has been communicated. It is a core element in preparing a successful transformation, and it needs to be given that role.
- ✓ **Does not overload the organization:** The 10x Results approach can be customized to fit perfectly with what your company needs.

10. Data Confirms the 10x Results Approach

"In God we trust; all others must bring data."
— W. Edwards Deming

To test and confirm the validity of the 10x Results approach, I reached out to business owners, CEOs, senior executives, and managers from around the world. As you can see from the table below, they came from companies of different sizes—from small to very large. They also came from diverse industries:

Representative Set of People Validating the 10x Results Approach

Position	Region	Industry	Company size (revenue)
Other	Africa	Other	More than $10 billion
CEO & similar	Australia/Oceania	Social & public sector	
	Latin America	Chemicals, process ind.	
		Media & entertainment	$1 to $10 billion
Owner & similar	Asia	Transportation/logistics	
		Energy, oil/gas, utilities	
		Healthcare/pharma	
	Europe	Financial services	
Senior executive		Consumer goods/retail	$100 million to $1 billion
		Professional services	
	North America	Industrial goods/services	
Manager		Tech/telecom	Less than $100 million

(All columns total 100%)

In total, I tested the recommendations with 481 individual business leaders. I believe that this sample size and also the good representation of people from different industries, different company sizes, different positions, and different geographic regions can give us confidence in the validity of the findings.

The business owners, CEOs, senior executives, and managers were asked two questions: (1) *What are the biggest pain points in your company today?* and (2) *What are the best strategies to address the pain points and drive your company to full potential?* Using these questions, I tested a broad set of potential value drivers. From this broad set of value drivers, I distilled it down to the few key strategies that really drive performance. These are also the measures that are presented in this book.

In the process, I also found out that many of the strategies that are typically employed like massive cost-cutting or embarking on large-scale acquisitions do not consistently yield great results.

THE MOST SIGNIFICANT PAIN POINTS IN MOST COMPANIES TODAY

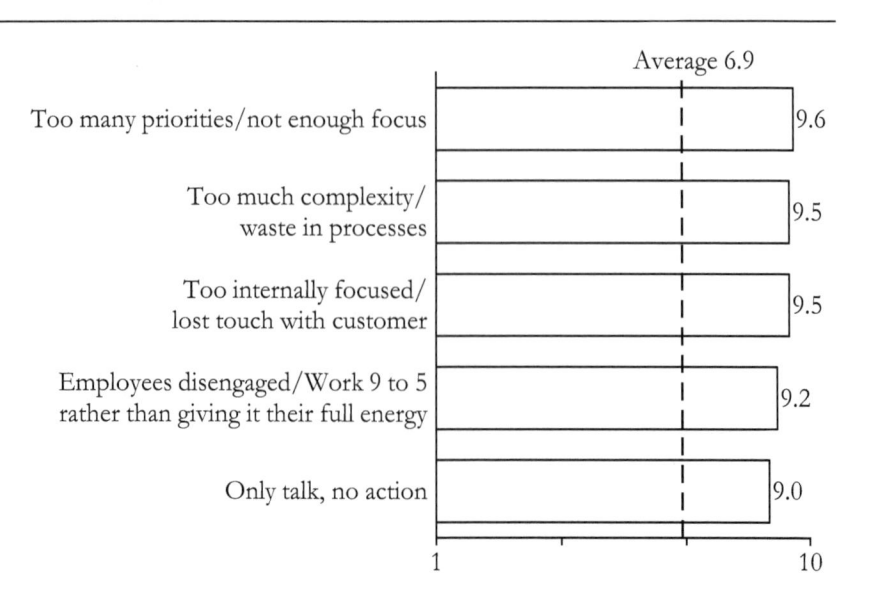

Pain Point	Score (Average 6.9)
Too many priorities/not enough focus	9.6
Too much complexity/waste in processes	9.5
Too internally focused/lost touch with customer	9.5
Employees disengaged/Work 9 to 5 rather than giving it their full energy	9.2
Only talk, no action	9.0

The questions were asked on a 1 to 10 scale, with 10 being the highest. As was expected, the respondents tended to agree with most of the pain points presented in the survey, which also moved the average across all responses more toward the upper end of the scale (6.9).

The same was true for the second question about the best strategies to drive the business to full potential. Also here, the average across all responses was more toward the upper end of the scale (7.1).

THE BEST STRATEGIES/LEVERS TO REACH FULL POTENTIAL IN MOST COMPANIES TODAY

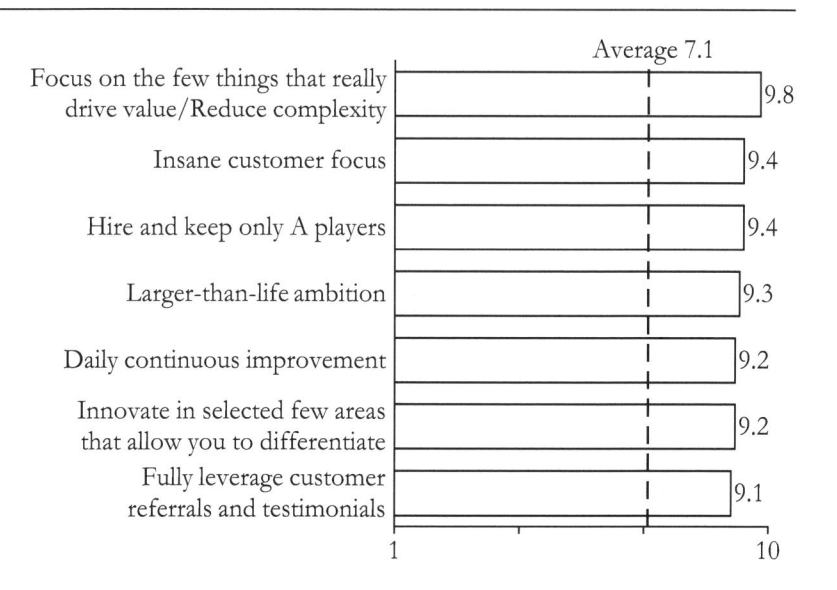

Average 7.1

Strategy	Score
Focus on the few things that really drive value/Reduce complexity	9.8
Insane customer focus	9.4
Hire and keep only A players	9.4
Larger-than-life ambition	9.3
Daily continuous improvement	9.2
Innovate in selected few areas that allow you to differentiate	9.2
Fully leverage customer referrals and testimonials	9.1

The findings are consistent across industries. They are also largely consistent across managerial levels. At the same time, there are significant differences between larger and smaller companies. While all identified strategies are important for both large and small companies, the larger companies saw the challenges more in remaining focused on the few things that really drive value, on fighting complexity and cutting waste, and on regaining an insane customer focus. For smaller companies, the key challenges were more in achieving profitable growth, maturing the processes and making them stable so that they could consistently deliver high quality, and hiring and keeping the best employees that they could find.

TOP THREE VALUE DRIVERS DIFFER BETWEEN LARGER AND SMALLER COMPANIES

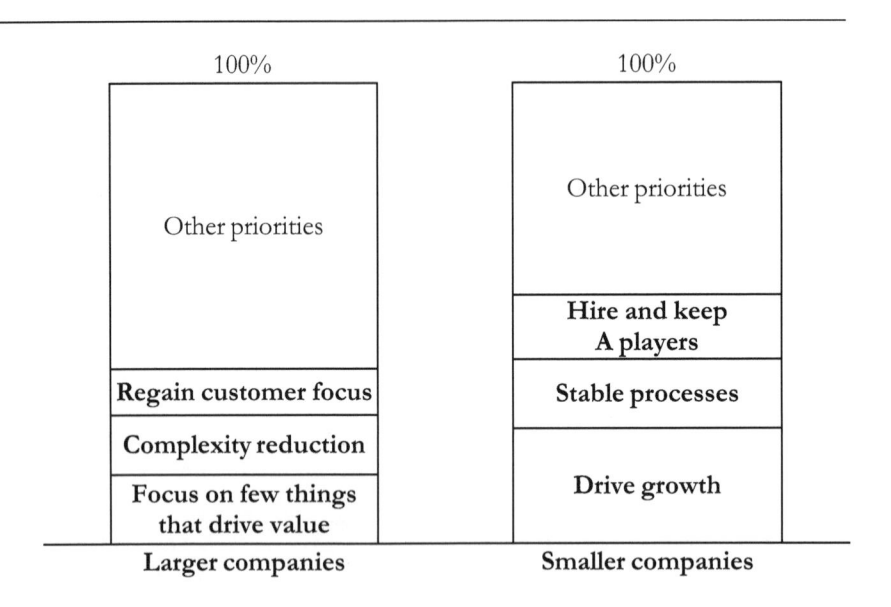

Larger companies	Smaller companies
Other priorities (100%)	Other priorities (100%)
Regain customer focus	Hire and keep A players
Complexity reduction	Stable processes
Focus on few things that drive value	Drive growth

As you will see in the closing chapters of this book, the 10x Results approach accounts well for the special situations of smaller and larger companies.

In summary, I am confident that the data confirms and supports the recommendations in this book. We will now move to the next sections, where I will explain each of the individual initiatives that will help you realize the full potential of your business.

THE FOUNDATION

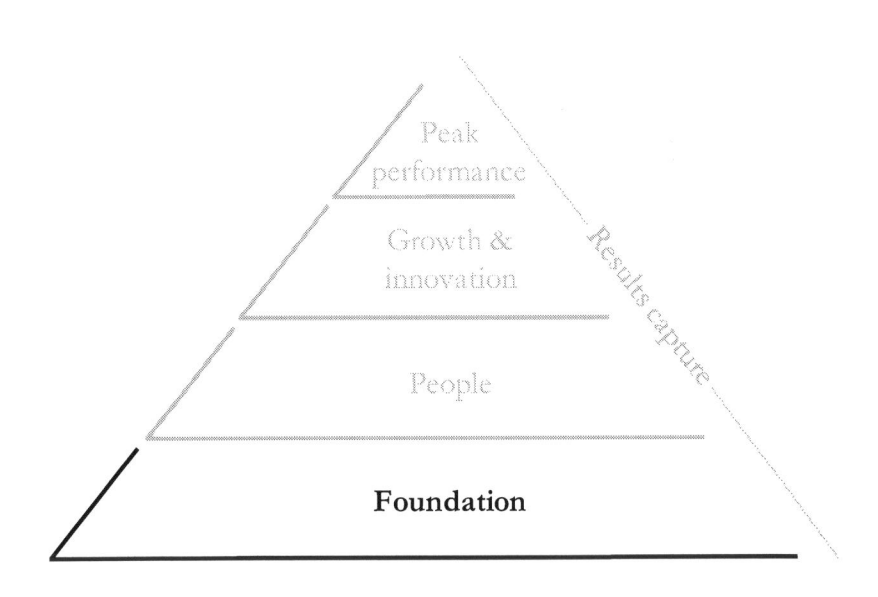

```
            Peak
         performance
                           Results capture
       Growth &
       innovation

         People

       Foundation
```

11. Focus, Focus, Focus

> *"That's been one of my mantras—focus and simplicity. Simple can be harder than complex: You have to work hard to get your thinking clean to make it simple. But it's worth it in the end because once you get there, you can move mountains."*
>
> — Steve Jobs

When I was a little boy, my father taught me one of the most important lessons of my life. My friends and I were playing in the yard. We had just learned to correctly hit a nail on the head with a hammer, and we were on the lookout for any kind of wood that we could find to put a nail in. It was fun, but we did not really produce anything of value. Then my father suggested that we build a small boat. He helped us with the design and picking of the wood, and by the end of the day, my friends and I had assembled our first boat. It was not the most beautiful boat, but we were still as proud as little boys can be. What an accomplishment!

The next day, we took the boat to a little pond nearby and put it in the water. It stayed afloat; we were very proud of ourselves. Now, I have to add that, ultimately, the boat sunk. We were standing up to our knees in water, but this is not the point. The next day we improved the design and got better and better at it. The point (or lesson) that I learned from this is if you focus your efforts, then you can achieve great things that surprise you and the people around you. But if you just continue to put nails into every piece of wood that you find, then nothing great will happen.

> ## 10X RESULTS "MILLION $ IDEA"
>
> IF YOU TRY TO BE GREAT IN TOO MANY AREAS (PRODUCT LINES, CUSTOMER SEGMENTS, DISTRIBUTION CHANNELS, ETC.), YOU WILL, AT BEST, **BECOME AVERAGE** IN MOST OF THEM. YOU WILL **BECOME INDISTINGUISHABLE** FROM THE COMPETITION: AVERAGE PRODUCT, AVERAGE CUSTOMER SERVICE, AVERAGE MARKETING.
>
> YOU NEED AN **EXCEPTIONAL** PRODUCT WITH **EXCEPTIONAL** MARKETING WITH **EXCEPTIONAL** PEOPLE WHO PROVIDE **EXCEPTIONAL** CUSTOMER SERVICE TO WIN BIG IN ANY MARKET.
>
> THE WAY TO BECOME EXCEPTIONAL IS TO **FOCUS ALL YOUR EFFORTS, TALENTS, RESOURCES, AND MONEY** ON THE PRODUCTS, CUSTOMER SEGMENTS, AND DISTRIBUTION CHANNELS WHERE YOU CAN BECOME TRULY EXCEPTIONAL.

Apple is probably one of the best case studies on the focus principle. In the late '80s and early '90s when Apple was continually increasing its product lines, it became more and more indistinguishable from the competition. It took the return of Steve Jobs and the radical reduction of Apple's product portfolio to return the company to profitable growth.

In the checklist below, I have listed a few questions that you may ask yourself to get started on your "focus journey."

CHECKLIST: WHERE TO FOCUS

- ✓ **Make our buy:** Apple focuses mainly on product design and marketing, but has other companies do the manufacturing. Ask yourself, which elements of the value chain help you truly differentiate yourself from the competition? In which areas can you become world class? And in which areas can other companies do an equally good (or often better) job? Look at outsourcing those activities. Don't keep doing things where you are average or even sub-par.
- ✓ **Product/service lines:** What market shares do each of your key product lines have in their respective markets? Are you the market leader (or at least among the top three)? Can you get there over the next three to five years? If not, try focusing on profitable sub-segments of the market or divesting the product/service line altogether. The market leader (Mercedes, Google, Amazon) reaps the big benefits. The followers (and especially distant followers) hardly break even.
- ✓ **Customer segments:** Do you cater to retail customers? Or business customers? Or large corporations? Or all of them? The skills that it takes to win in each of these segments, and even sub-segments within them, are very different. That starts with different pricing and service strategies and ends with sales approach plus marketing message. If you can pull all of this off, then good for you. But most companies can't. Most companies would benefit hugely from focusing on a few, well-picked customer segments. Look at companies like BMW, Nordstrom, or Schlumberger.

There is one important caveat to add. As you start investigating whether to move out of particular customer segments or product lines, you also need to look at the degree of cost sharing or customer sharing between your product lines. Otherwise, it could happen that as you move away from that particular product line, you are still stuck with certain fixed costs (e.g., production line), but on a much-reduced revenue base. This will negatively impact your profitability. The same will happen when customers who used to buy product bundles from you switch to the competition after you have removed an essential product from that bundle. These adverse effects can be offset by careful transitioning over time or sourcing the missing product from a third party to still sell the bundle.

10X RESULTS "MILLION $ IDEA"

IF A LASER IS NOT FOCUSED, IT IS WEAK; IF THE LASER LIGHT IS FOCUSED, IT CAN DO INCREDIBLE THINGS.

IN YOUR NEXT MANAGEMENT MEETING, HAVE A DISCUSSION WITH YOUR TEAM ON THE AREAS WHERE YOU ARE (OR CAN BECOME) TRULY WORLD CLASS. AND EVEN MORE IMPORTANT, HAVE AN HONEST DEBATE ON WHAT THIS MEANS FOR THE OTHER AREAS OF THE COMPANY. KIMBERLY-CLARK BECAME A GREAT COMPANY A FEW DECADES BACK WHEN THEY HAD A FRANK DISCUSSION ON HOW TO PROCEED WITH THE PAPER MANUFACTURING BUSINESS.

One of the most critical roles of leaders in any organization is to help their team focus on the few key things/priorities that really move the needle. In your company, what are the "three must-win battles?" Which one or two strategic initiatives do you need to set in motion to win these "three must-win battles"? Overcommunicate these initiatives; have the organization live and breathe them. This creates a laser focus on the initiatives, and this is what leads to extraordinary results.

MOVING TO ACTION: QUESTIONS TO ASK YOURSELF

- ✓ What are the areas in your business where you are world class (or can become world class)? How can you leverage these areas to position your overall products and services as truly world class? How can you use these areas to charge premium prices?
- ✓ What are the areas in your business where you are average or even sub-par? What is your strategy here? Can you turn these areas around? Or source them from a supplier who is world class?

12. Reduce Complexity and Cut Waste

> *"Any intelligent fool can make things bigger, more complex, and more violent. It takes a touch of genius — and a lot of courage to move in the opposite direction."*
> — Albert Einstein/Ernst F. Schumacher

This chapter goes hand in hand with the previous chapter. In many ways, cutting complexity and waste is the "twin sister" of focusing on what really matters.

Complexity reduction is not a onetime thing. You need to review the complexity in your business at least every other year. It's a little bit like losing weight. Sometime in the spring, you realize that you are not yet "beach body" material. So, you exercise and shed those few extra pounds. You enjoy your beach body during the summer months, but by the time November comes, you have again put on a few extra pounds that are nicely hidden by warm clothing. The longer you wait and get comfy, the harder it will be to get back in shape again.

We start off this chapter with two tables that detail areas of complexity and waste in both management and production processes. Please review the lists and see which points apply to your company.

I suggest that you also talk to some of your middle managers and more junior people in the organization. They are often better at spotting complexity and waste than your senior executive colleagues.

Checklist: Areas of Hidden Complexity and Waste in Management Processes

- ✓ **Reports:** If you were to go to any major corporation and print out all the reports that get produced in a day, you would likely end up with a pile that is several meters high. And most of these reports will never be read (at least not in the detail in which they are produced), and yet they overcrowd email inboxes. This is waste on both ends: For the people creating the reports and for the people who are supposed to read them. If you are short on people or need an instant boost in your productivity, do a zero-based review of all reports and cut down aggressively. You will likely see that you really only need 20 to 30 percent of the reports that are currently being produced. Keep those, and put the resources that you freed up to better, more productive use.

- ✓ **Functional overlap:** If you have more than five to seven functional heads sitting on your management Board, then you likely have a functional complexity issue. You will notice this when for almost any topic that needs to be discussed, three to four of your functional heads need to get involved. And then they need to loop in their direct reports and so on. This creates an enormous number of meetings and conference calls that would not be necessary if you combined your functional head roles (ideally five or at max seven). You will see that processes run much smoother. One personal example to illustrate: When I was on the Europe Management Board of a Fortune 100 company, I was overseeing strategy, BPO, customer service, and transformation. Now, imagine what would happen if there would be individual heads for all these roles. Right—you get my point.

- ✓ **Management layers:** Some 10 to 15 years ago there was a considerable push to cut management layers in most companies. Looking at the current organizational structures in many companies, I sense that in many places new layers have been added back in. In my opinion, there is hardly ever a reason to have a managerial role if this person has only two direct reports, even if this person performs the managerial tasks on top of his or her regular activities. This leads to micro-teams and functional overlap and complexity. My experience is that for most "thinking roles" a manager should ideally have somewhere between seven and 10 direct reports. For call center or production line roles, this can go well above 15 or even 20 direct reports. For all other roles, it would be somewhere in between. I know that cleaning up these ineffective and inefficient structures will lead to an uproar in middle management. I also appreciate that some of your key talent may be parked in those roles. But if they are indeed your key talent, you will find other suitable roles where they can develop their full potential until they are ready to take on responsibilities for larger teams. I personally advocate for the concept of informal deputy roles; this allows the talent to be groomed in a safe and functioning environment.

- ✓ **Legacy functions:** Some positions or even functions may have been created 10 to 20 years back for a specific reason. Today, even if the reason for having this position or function is no longer valid, they will still be around, and they will create unnecessary work for themselves and for others (to appear busy). Take out these functions and deploy the resources where they add much more value.

CHECKLIST: AREAS OF HIDDEN COMPLEXITY AND WASTE IN PRODUCTION PROCESSES

- ✓ **Defects:** Defects lead to additional efforts (time and money) to fix them. The worst and most costly case would be a return

from the customer. Not only will you have additional costs for transportation, channels, and the like, you will also have eroded the trust of the customer in your products. This can easily be the hardest defect to repair.
- ✓ **Overproduction, inventories, waiting time:** Inventories (be it raw materials, semi-finished goods, or finished goods) are tying up capital that can be put to better use elsewhere. Now, I understand that *just in time* is difficult in many places and that some inventories are typically required, but keep them to a minimum to balance inventory costs and the risk for running out of stock. Another area of waste is waiting time. This can be in the form of waiting for the next production step or waiting for the next shift to arrive. Try to keep waiting to a minimum.
- ✓ **Motion and transportation:** Poor production floor layout creates extra motion of people, equipment, and production materials.

Over the past almost 30 years since the release of the book *The Machine that Changed the World* by Womack et al. about the Toyota Production System, many advances have been made to take out complexity and waste in production and managerial processes. Most companies now have some kind of *lean* or *Six Sigma* program to address these issues.

The problem that I see in my daily life is that these programs have led to institutionalized teams that administer them, but overall they have become more of a burden to the organization than a help. It does not have to be that way. Make the task of complexity and waste reduction a responsibility of all your people in their day-to-day work. Do not create large programs with even more bureaucracy. Instead, make it easy for your people to implement small improvements in their daily work quickly and with little bureaucracy.

> ## 10x Results "Million $ Idea"
>
> **Cost reduction programs can be a very effective way to reduce complexities and cut waste.** The key for this to work is to set the savings targets high enough so that your teams can no longer create the same output by merely working harder.
>
> Let's assume you set the headcount reduction target to 20 percent and explain thoroughly why it needs to be this high. Then you **ask your team the following questions:**
>
> **(1) Which activities should we stop doing?**
>
> **(2) Which activities should we do differently to get the same or even better result with much less effort?**
>
> **(3) How can we optimize the overall process flows to reduce waste** (e.g., handovers between departments)?
>
> One way to do this is to **identify the people who you take out from the team early, and then have the remainder of the group present their proposal** on how to address these questions. You will be impressed with what your team comes back with.

It makes a lot of sense to repeat this cost/complexity/waste reduction process every three to five years to keep your organization lean and focused. Some companies even do it every two years.

One more thing: Cutting complexity and waste does not necessarily mean laying off people. Don't get me wrong, continuously reviewing the performance of your people and managing out the bottom 5 percent each year is a very good thing. It keeps the organization agile and effective.

But layoffs as a result of complexity reduction reviews affect not just your bottom performers, but all of your people. And letting go of some of your best people just because they happen to work in an area that is no longer needed would be one of the most wasteful activities. You have invested a lot of time and money to get your people trained, and now you are letting them go (and even paying additional money for that). Instead, redeploy those top performers to other activities that generate much more value.

Complexity reduction reviews are also beneficial in situations where your company is in a high-growth industry, but you have difficulties finding the right people on the market to sustain that growth. In these cases, you can use this methodology to help keep your company growing without excessively adding personnel (that you may not even be able to find).

10x Results "Million $ Idea"

One of the most important things that any company needs to master is operational excellence or "getting their processes under control."

Having **(1) simple processes with as little as possible handover points that (2) deliver the expected outcome consistently with de facto no process failures** is the key to business success and customer happiness. What you want is a **repeatable model that delivers the same results every time** (even independent of the people who work in the processes).

The Foundation

> For example, in the restaurant business, it does not help you to serve exceptional food and have exceptional service once and then fail miserably when your customers come back for more. Your food and service need to be **exceptional all the time.**
>
> One more thing: **Do not "bastardize" your processes.** Some companies keep on adding complexities to their processes to cater to special cases or customer demands. This will lead to a much higher risk of process failures and costs.

One thought on IT: Process automation through IT is a great thing. But it can only work when you have your processes under control in the first place. So, first get your processes stable and defect free; only then should you start putting IT automation on top of it.

I want to close this chapter with thoughts on business strategy and priorities. The reality in many companies is that there are way too many priorities and a business strategy that hardly anyone below top management understands, let alone can articulate. This is a pity. A clear strategy supported by a few key priorities that everybody in the company understands can be extremely powerful to help focus the organization and get it moving in the right direction. The box below may help you get started on this.

> ## 10x Results "Million $ Idea"
>
> Ideally, your **strategy should fit on one page.**
>
> It should articulate **(1) which customers you serve, (2) which of their pains you help cure with your prod-**

> **UCTS AND SERVICES, (3) IN WHICH SPECIFIC WAYS THAT MATTER TO CUSTOMERS YOU DO THIS BETTER THAN THE COMPETITION, AND (4) WHAT THE ROLE OF EACH OF YOUR EMPLOYEES IS IN THIS.** THIS SHOULD BE SUPPORTED BY A LIST OF THE **THREE KEY PRIORITIES OR "MUST-WIN BATTLES"** THAT EVERYBODY IN THE COMPANY NEEDS TO FULLY SUPPORT TO REALIZE THIS STRATEGY.
>
> THIS IS ALL IT TAKES. PUT THIS IN SIMPLE, EMOTIONAL WORDS, AND COMMUNICATE IT OVER AND OVER AGAIN.

MOVING TO ACTION: QUESTIONS TO ASK YOURSELF

- ✓ What are some quick-win, no-regret areas of complexity in your business that you can take out (e.g., excessive reports)? Do it today (to start the process and get the organization moving in the right direction).
- ✓ Ask each of your management colleagues to identify 10 areas of significant complexity and waste in the company's current processes. Ask them to come up with suggestions on how to address these. Ask them also to come up with a first ballpark, impact estimate (cost savings, time savings, quality improvements).

13. Insane Customer Focus

> *"Success in business and success in life reflect the impact you have on the people around you, and on the quality of your relationships with them. [...] Enrich more lives, diminish fewer. In other words, create more promoters and fewer detractors. That is the way to ultimate success in your business and in your life."*
>
> — Fred Reichheld

Success in dating and success in business have many things in common. This is why I sometimes recommend the movie *Hitch* starring Will Smith to salespeople who want to become better at their job.

First and foremost, success at selling is a question of attitude: You need to listen. You need to try to understand the other person—his or her pains, ambitions, dreams. You need to make yourself vulnerable so that an emotional connection can be established.

Jumping over these crucial first steps will not get you a second or third date, and will also likely not get you the sale.

10x Results "Million $ Idea"

Many large companies have turned inward-looking. Eighty percent of the staff have not spoken to a single customer over the past 12 months. And even the salespeople invest half of their time creating sales reports for middle and top management instead of talking to customers.

> **YOU NEED TO BREAK THIS CYCLE:** TRY TO **HAVE ALL OF YOUR EMPLOYEES EXPOSED TO THE VOICE OF THE CUSTOMER** AT LEAST ONCE EVERY QUARTER. BRING CUSTOMERS TO COMPANY EVENTS, HAVE THEM ATTEND AND SPEAK IN ALL-HANDS MEETINGS. MANY OF YOUR PEOPLE MAY INITIALLY BE SHY TO TALK TO CUSTOMERS, BUT ONCE THEY UNDERSTAND THAT CUSTOMERS ARE PEOPLE AS WELL—WITH FEELINGS AND DREAMS—THEY WILL BECOME MUCH BETTER AT THEIR JOBS. BECAUSE THEY WILL UNDERSTAND "WHAT CUSTOMERS REALLY WANT."

Coming back to the dating example helps illustrate this point: A sale is always a situation where the customer puts himself or herself on the line. The customer has a significant problem to solve and puts his faith in your hands. He needs to be able to trust that your product or service will indeed solve the problem. This same principle is at work when a person considers marrying you (putting his or her future life into your hands). Understanding this emotional angst in your customer and relating to it will greatly increase your effectiveness in any sales situation.

> ## 10x RESULTS "MILLION $ IDEA"
>
> CUSTOMERS **NEVER** BUY PURELY BASED ON PRICE. SAYING THAT CUSTOMERS ONLY LOOK AT PRICE IS DANGEROUS AND A LAZY EXCUSE BY SOME SALESPEOPLE. THE SALES PROCESS—EVEN FOR PRODUCTS LIKE SCREWS OR SAUSAGES—CAN BE HIGHLY EMOTIONAL. AND **THE MORE YOU CAN AMPLIFY THESE EMOTIONS, THE MORE UNIQUE YOUR PRODUCT BECOMES AND THE MORE AT A PREMIUM YOU CAN SELL IT.**

> Look at companies like Wurth, Ben & Jerry's, or even Starbucks.
>
> **Action item: Brainstorm with your team about how you can "emotionalize" your products** in the eyes of the customer. Ask them **what it would take to keep the customer even if you were 10, 20, or 30 percent more expensive than the competition** (solution design/features, marketing, loyalty program, partnerships). This discussion can lead to real breakthroughs in how you position your products and services (and what profit margin you can realize).

To get you started on building your "insane customer focus" and listening more directly to customers, I recommend the "Net Promoter Approach" to you. This concept was popularized by Fred Reichheld in his book *The Ultimate Question*. After a lot of research and testing, Fred figured out that asking customers the following question helps best in driving up sales and identifying problems early on:

> ## 10x Results "Million $ Idea"
>
> Ask your customers after every major interaction, **"How likely is it that you would recommend our company/product/service to a friend or colleague on a scale of 0 to 10** (with 10 being the highest)?"
>
> Customers who answer with a 9 or 10 are called **promoters, who are likely to buy more, remain more loyal, and make referrals.** Customers who respond with a 0 to 6 are called **detractors who are at high risk of leav-**

> **ING FOR THE COMPETITION OR EVEN BAD-MOUTHING YOU.** CUSTOMERS WITH A SCORE OF 7 OR 8 ARE NEUTRAL (YOU SEE THAT IN THIS SCALE THE NEUTRAL POINT IS SLIGHTLY SKEWED).
>
> THE **NET PROMOTER SCORE (NPS)** IS CALCULATED BY SUBTRACTING THE PERCENTAGE OF CUSTOMERS WHO ARE DETRACTORS FROM THE PERCENTAGE OF CUSTOMERS WHO ARE PROMOTERS.

If you follow up this question with a "why" question, then you will gain valuable insights on how to improve your products, services, and processes. This is one of the most effective and direct ways to remain close to the customer and drive business growth.

One final thought on customer research and focus groups: Sometimes their results are misleading. Often it is better to develop a "minimum viable product" and get it out to market quickly. This will allow you to get real-time, real customer feedback and then improve the product/service based on it.

MOVING TO ACTION: QUESTIONS TO ASK YOURSELF

- ✓ How can you ensure that all people in your company get to hear "the voice of the customer?"
- ✓ How can you ensure that you get frequent and direct customer feedback? Does it make sense to implement the Net Promoter Approach?
- ✓ How can you leverage this customer feedback to differentiate your products and services in the eyes of your customers? Sometimes, even small tweaks in your marketing message or in your product features will allow you to clearly differentiate your products and services, and consequently, charge premium prices.

14. Getting Better Every Day

"It's not the big things that add up in the end; it's the hundreds, thousands, or millions of little things that separate the ordinary from the extraordinary."
— Darren Hardy

British cycling was nowhere in the early 2000s. All they could show was one Olympic gold medal in more than 50 years. Then, they won a total of 22 Olympic gold medals at the Games of 2008, 2012, and 2016. How did they accomplish this feat?

According to Sir David Brailsford, the head of British cycling for most of this period, the reason for this success was a mindset of continually seeking small improvements in all areas possible. In an interview with *Harvard Business Review* (HBR), he commented on the details: (1) small improvements in aerodynamics, (2) teaching cyclists how to wash their hands properly so they would not become ill as often, (3) keeping the truck that carried the bikes clean from dust, (4) ensuring high-quality nutrition, and (5) having cyclists bring their own mattresses and pillows to the races to ensure sound sleep.

How does this relate to you and your company? It is rarely the big "bet-the-company" moves that lead to sustained value creation. Announcing a multibillion dollar acquisition may make the headlines of the *Wall Street Journal* and *Financial Times*, but as many studies have proven far more than half of all mergers and acquisitions fail to deliver on their initial promises. So, what is the better alternative?

> ## 10x Results "Million $ Idea"
>
> **Seeking constant, small improvements in your day-to-day work may not be sexy and may not allow you to make the headlines** of major newspapers. **But this is what will allow you to far outperform your competitors.**
>
> Some examples of small improvements are: Measuring your win rates in RFQs, then figuring out why you lost and addressing these root causes; addressing production quality problems once they pop up (and not only when customers start complaining); measuring employee engagement and finding ways to further improve it; taking out waste in business processes and focusing the company on a few priorities. **Improvement in these small areas combined over time is what ultimately makes you successful.**
>
> This process is like the steps in a staircase. Jumping to the roof of a building that is 10 stories tall is something nobody can do. But taking the stairs one step at a time is something everybody can do. And before long, you will be standing at the rooftop.

There are many areas where you can look for small improvements. I suggest that when launching the "small improvements effort," you focus on a few areas where you expect the most to be gained (e.g., sales effectiveness, product quality, and marketing). Do not try to do everything at once. You need early, visible successes so that your people see the value of this effort and adopt it themselves.

Below is a table with a few thoughts that may help get you started with this process.

CHECKLIST: SOME IDEAS ON WHERE TO LOOK FOR CONTINUOUS IMPROVEMENT OPPORTUNITIES

- ✓ **Sales pipeline—prospecting:** Is your pipeline filled with HIGH-quality prospects? How can you improve the quality and quantity of your prospects while maintaining the size of your sales team?
- ✓ **Sales pipeline—closing the deal:** Analyze the times when you were most successful in closing the deal? Why? How can you replicate this behavior with the other deals?
- ✓ **Product marketing:** Does your marketing allow you to clearly stand out from any competing products? Is it memorable? Does it lead to action?
- ✓ **Product quality:** What are the root causes of product quality failure? How can you fix them?

Again, I am not advocating against large, bold moves to reorient the company to a brighter future. Instead, I am arguing to make much more use of improvement opportunities in seemingly small areas that, when added up, lead to significant improvements overall.

Ultimately, the mindset of looking for small improvements in your day-to-day work needs to be top of mind for all employees. Whenever they see something that can be done better, they should take the initiative to do so. This way, when you consider all the small improvements by everybody throughout the weeks and months and years together, you will see amazing results.

Moving to Action: Questions to Ask Yourself

- ✓ How can you institutionalize processes of continuous daily improvement?
- ✓ **Which areas** for continuous improvement **should you initially focus on** in order not to "boil the ocean," but get tangible results quickly?
- ✓ How can you make sure that this **indeed yields value** and does not become a bureaucratic monster?

15. Measure Success

> *"What gets measured gets managed."*
> — Peter Drucker

"What are the five to seven key metrics that will determine your company's success six months from now?" Pause for a moment and try to answer this question. Do you know exactly what these five to seven key metrics are? I am not talking about current revenue or profit figures, I am talking about lead KPIs that will determine what revenues and profits you will make in a few months. Do you know how you are stacking up against each of these metrics at any given moment (without looking them up on your laptop)? Do you review and discuss them with your team in the monthly management meetings?

Can you answer all of these questions with a resounding "yes?" If so, good for you. But if you are like most executives, then you may have had problems naming the right lead KPIs that will drive most of your success six months from now. And this may be one of the reasons why your company is not as successful today as it could be.

10x Results "Million $ Idea"

ONE OF THE MOST IMPORTANT PREREQUISITES FOR ANY BUSINESS TO SUCCEED IS TO **BE CRYSTAL CLEAR ON WHAT THE FIVE TO SEVEN KEY LEAD INDICATORS ARE THAT WILL DETERMINE YOUR BUSINESS SUCCESS SIX TO 12 MONTHS FROM NOW.**

> **Hint:** It is not EBIT or revenues or EBITDA or FCF. It could be metrics like (1) Business Pipeline Growth/Volume, (2) Net Promoter Score, (3) Involuntary Employee Attrition, and (4) Shipment Returns.
>
> Once you have identified these five to seven key lead indicators, you need to track them and manage them. Then, the rest will take care of itself.

A few things are important to mention: I picked the numbers five to seven for a reason. Most businesses make the mistake of either tracking too many numbers and then getting lost in the weeds, or too few numbers (e.g., only revenue and EBIT). In my experience, I found that five to seven key lead indicators are about the right amount for a company that operates mainly in one business area; enough to get a nuanced view, yet not too many so that you lose focus of what is really important. Typically, you will find three to four sales and customer-related metrics and two to three metrics that relate to operations (including employees). Every additional business that you operate in will add another two to three metrics to your list.

Let me give you an example to illustrate: Let's assume you want to lose 10 pounds over the next three months. A bad indicator would be the number of pounds since it is not a lead indicator and also not actionable. Much better lead indicators would be:

- Minutes of physical exercise per day with a pulse between 115 and 130 bpm (target: 30)
- Steps per day (target: 15,000)
- Share of healthy (e.g., fresh food, veggies, low carbs and sugar, good fats, water) versus unhealthy (e.g., fast food, candy bars, Coke, beer, chips) meals per week (target: more than 90 percent)

- Early time to bed (before 10 p.m.) and long enough time in bed (no less than seven hours of sleep) per week (target: 6 weekdays)

Many fitness trackers allow you to easily monitor the metrics mentioned above—and for the food, you can keep an easy journal. All in all, the tracking effort should take no more than three minutes per day, and you should see visible improvements in your body weight and posture within the first few weeks.

Now, the question, of course, is how to identify the five to seven key lead indicators for your business:

CHECKLIST: HOW TO IDENTIFY THE FIVE TO SEVEN KEY LEAD INDICATORS FOR YOUR BUSINESS

- ✓ **Start at the top:** Ask "what does it take to be successful in our business?" You may get answers like: loyal customers, business growth based on customer referrals, innovative products that create customer hype, smart and loyal employees, strong brand recognition, highest product quality.
- ✓ **Peel the onion:** Next, try to dig two to three levels deeper and understand what exactly drives each of these topics and how you can measure them. For "loyal customers," you may arrive at the Net Promoter Score (NPS) as the key metric. For business growth, you may arrive at the number of referrals per promoter per quarter as the key metric, and so on.
- ✓ **Test the first hypothesis:** Test the first hypothesis on the five to seven key lead indicators using historical data from one to two years ago. Do these figures predict your current performance? Or is the link weak? Then adjust, fine-tune, and repeat the testing until you have indicators with good predictability.

These five to seven metrics is what you should keep top of mind every day. With every business decision that you make, you should ask yourself: "How will this decision affect each of these metrics? How can I further drive them up? What can I do to avoid any downside risk?"

It provides you with a lot of focus and mental clarity when you are able to boil down the inner workings of your business model to a few key metrics that you need to track. And not only does it provide focus and clarity to you, it does the same for your team and investors.

MOVING TO ACTION: QUESTIONS TO ASK YOURSELF

- ✓ What are the five to seven key lead indicators in your business? Brainstorm and validate the list with your management team.
- ✓ Are they easy enough to measure and easy enough to understand (i.e., are you able to communicate them to your frontline employees and to investors)?
- ✓ How will you display them visibly in your office (tracking monthly performance over time)?
- ✓ How do you integrate them into your regular discussions with your management team?

16. Bias for Action

> *"My attitude has always been, if you fall flat on your face, at least you're moving forward. All you have to do is get back up and try again [...] Treat failure as a lesson on how not to approach achieving a goal and then use that learning to improve your chances of success when you try again. Failure is only the end if you decide to stop."*
> — Richard Branson

Think back on the last 10 years. Take a sheet of paper and make two columns. On the left, jot down the big failures that you experienced in your professional life over those 10 years. Now, on the right, write down the missed opportunities that you regret. Did you act too late? Or did you not act at all? I bet that the right-hand side of your paper with the missed opportunities is much longer than the left-hand side.

When I did this exercise for myself, the missed opportunities list was about three times as long as the big failure list. Back in the day, I was proud of myself for not making many mistakes. But now at an older age, I realize that my risk minimization strategy came at a very high cost. Don't make the same mistake.

The case that I want to build here is that we all follow a bit more the example of Richard Branson who named one of his books *Screw It, Let's Do It*. With this, I by no means advocate that we become reckless—that we just blindly pursue any opportunity that pops up. Instead, I want to make the case that after careful analysis and weighting of all the pros and cons, we take action and try out new business ideas. Maybe it will work, and perhaps you will win big.

Let's make this more concrete.

> ## 10x Results "Million $ Idea"
>
> With your top management team, **brainstorm ways to take your company to the next level.** Do not evaluate the ideas initially.
>
> Then, jointly **agree on the five to 10 most promising ideas.** This could be that you leverage social media as a sales channel much more. Or that you enter a new country. Or that you open an adjacent product line. Or that you enter into a partnership agreement that gives you access to a new customer segment.
>
> Next, assign one of these promising ideas to each of your Board members to prepare **a small business plan (approach, funding, timeline, resources, risks, and mitigation steps).**
>
> And now the most crucial point: In your next Board meeting, **select the three most promising ideas and give them a try.**

None of these three promising ideas should be "bet-the-company" moves. They should all have considerable upside if they work out and a very controllable downside if things go south.

The benefit of this approach is that you are educating your people to take action even if not all the facts are on the table and even if some residual risks remain. You will, in any case, never be able to plan everything out from A to Z. Things will happen on the way, and you will have to react to them.

CHECKLIST: HOW TO REDUCE THE RISK OF FAILURE

- ✓ **What is the worst thing that could happen?** Get a second and third opinion on the plan; nominate people to play the devil's advocate role. Listen without commenting. Look at all the things that could go wrong (competitor moves, service failures, regulatory forces, recession, etc.).
- ✓ **How can we minimize the downside?** Brainstorm strategies to reduce the risks. Would you rather partner with another company than go it all alone? Can you hedge against any of the risks? Can certain risks be reduced with more detailed planning? Plan in what-if scenarios: "If this happens, what will we do to mitigate?" Put your best minds on developing this plan.
- ✓ **Small-scale experiments:** Don't bet the house. Large-scale bets like mergers or divesting the core business have a high risk of failure. Instead, do (a lot) of small experiments. Maybe they work out, or maybe not. Penicillin and x-rays were discovered more by accident than by design.

MOVING TO ACTION: QUESTIONS TO ASK YOURSELF

- ✓ What are the most promising opportunities for your company on the horizon?
- ✓ What is holding you back from doubling down on those opportunities?
- ✓ What are the best strategies to keep risks at acceptable levels?

17. Commit to a Goal and Stick to It When It Gets Tough

> *"Grit is that 'extra something' that separates the most successful people from the rest. It's the passion, perseverance, and stamina that we must channel in order to stick with our dreams until they become a reality."*
> — Travis Bradberry/Angela Duckworth

It almost ruined a formerly very successful company. Here is what happened: About 15 years ago, the company embarked on an ambitious digital transformation effort. They had operations in more than 100 countries around the world; the processes, IT systems, and business practices were very heterogeneous. The goal was to bring all core processes in all countries onto an integrated IT platform.

Long story short, four years into the transformation the efforts stalled. Shortly thereafter, they were rebooted with new management and a new target IT solution. The entire requirements gathering, solution design, and IT development work started from scratch. Only to stall again four years later. Another time, the management was changed, and the target solution was adjusted.

Over the course of these 15 years, the company, that was the envy of all competitors, lost market leadership in many important areas. It was largely internally focused over those 15 years. Now, what is the lesson?

> ## 10x Results "Million $ Idea"
>
> In any change effort, you will meet resistance—significant resistance. From employees, from investors, from your management team. You may even have doubts yourself.
>
> One of the worst things that can happen (and it happens often) is that halfway through the change, when the pain is highest, a new management team is brought in and the direction is changed. Only to find yourself in a similarly painful situation a few months down the line.
>
> This is **like trying to climb a mountain over and over again** (on different routes) and **each time stopping 100 yards before reaching the top.**
>
> **These repeated "episodes of pain" need to be avoided. If you are convinced that the change effort is still the right thing to do, then you have to see it through to the end.**
>
> So, it **becomes no longer a question of "If," but rather a question of "How"** best to do it. And in that case, there are excellent change management practices that can be applied.

I am not advocating that a failed transformation effort that is built on the wrong premises needs to be pushed through to the end. What I am advocating is that after careful analysis and when you and your management team still believe that it is the right thing to do, you have to endure the "episode of pain" and see the change effort through to the end.

To help you assess whether it is time to course-correct or not, I have listed a few "red flag" items in the table below:

CHECKLIST: WHEN TO COURSE-CORRECT YOUR CHANGE EFFORT

- ✓ **Too much to swallow:** One of the most common mistakes in any transformation is to try to do too much at the same time: cutting costs, bringing new products to market, implementing a new IT system, driving cultural change. You just cannot eat an apple in one bite. Therefore, the appropriate strategy is to chunk down the transformation into digestible bites. With each bite, the organization's "change muscle" becomes better trained. This will also allow you to swallow increasingly larger chunks of the apple.
- ✓ **Conditions change:** This could be changes in technology (for example, the envisioned solution is no longer state-of-the-art and would be outdated even before it is implemented). Or it could be changes in the market environment (recession, social unrest/revolution, new and stricter legislation).

So, let's assume that the market conditions did indeed change and the transformation effort needs to be adjusted significantly. This is one of the most challenging situations to be in. Not the least, because you have committed yourself personally to this transformation. Still, the best thing to do is to openly communicate to the team what has changed and that it would no longer be wise to pursue the transformation as planned.

At the same time you make this announcement, you need to also sketch out the new course of action. Your team (and the capital markets) will appreciate you even more for your courage to take this brave step and admit that you were mistaken. You will be seen as a mature and sensible leader who is able to course-correct when it is needed.

Moving to Action: Questions to Ask Yourself

- ✓ What are the transformation initiatives in your company where the implementation is stalling?
- ✓ Do you need to break down the initiatives to digestible bites? Do you need to better communicate? Or enlist multipliers within the organization who help carry and explain your message to everybody in the organization?
- ✓ Do you need to course-correct? Why? What is the new course? What makes you sure that this is the right one? How will you communicate the course-correction to your team and the capital markets?

18. Summary: Key Insights and Action Plan

Use these two pages to capture the thoughts, epiphanies, revenue and profit ideas that came to your head when reading the last couple of chapters. Take 20 minutes to jot down the ideas. You will find that this time is very well invested. We will refer to this summary at the end of the book.

Book Section: "The Foundation"

My Action Plan

- ✓ Epiphanies/aha moments from this section: ……………..
  ………………………………………..………………………………
  ………………………………………………………………………
  ………………………………………………………………………
  ………………………………………………………………………
  ………………………………………………………………………
  ………………………………………………………………………
  ………………………………………………………………………
  ………………………………………………………………………
  ………………………………………………………………………

- ✓ What I will immediately start implementing with my team as of next Monday morning: ……………………………..
  ……………………………………………………………………..

....
....
....
....
....
....
....
....
....

- ✓ Game-changing ideas that require thought and careful preparation. Assign a Board member to prepare a proposal on how to best implement/capture max benefits: ....
....
....
....
....
....
....
....
....
....
....
....

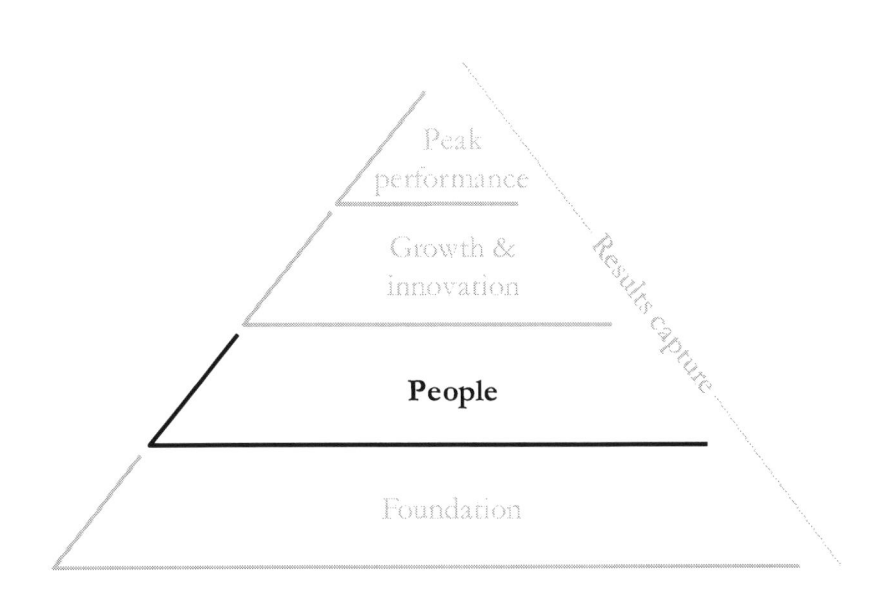

MULTIPLY THE PRODUCTIVITY OF YOUR PEOPLE

19. Give Your Team a "Why" That Is Worth Fighting for

> *"Very few people or companies can clearly articulate WHY they do WHAT they do. By WHY I mean your purpose, cause or belief. WHY does your company exist? WHY do you get out of bed every morning? And WHY should anyone care?"*
>
> — Simon Sinek

Why does a young man decide to join the military and fight for his country? Why does a young woman choose to join a non-profit organization and put in long hours at minimum pay? Why does a young teacher decide to work in one of the worst neighborhoods in the country?

Because they all see a deeper meaning in what they are doing. They believe that what they are doing each day will make a true difference in the lives of others. This sense of mission, this sense of purpose is what you should be aiming for in your employees as well.

Unfortunately, the reality in most companies is different. Many employees go through the workday with a motivation of 3 to 5 on a 10-point scale. Yes, they do their work. And yes, they also like their work. But they do not burn for it, fight for it, go the extra mile. Imagine what your company would look like if you could raise the motivation level by just three points to a 6 to 8 on a 10-point scale? Imagine if your people would take initiative, go the extra mile, or put their hearts into their work.

Most people are inspired by doing good for other people (and in the process also doing good for themselves, both financially and non-financially). Even in some of the most money-centered and competitive industries (like hedge funds or investment banking), this can be done very successfully, as Ray Dalio of Bridgewater Associates has proven.

> ### 10x RESULTS "MILLION $ IDEA"
>
> **IF YOU CAN GIVE YOUR TEAM A "WHY" THAT INSPIRES THEM,** YOU WILL SEE THAT THEY WILL DELIVER MUCH MORE GREAT WORK FOR YOU.
>
> **INSTILL A SENSE OF PURPOSE, A SENSE OF MISSION IN YOUR EMPLOYEES. GIVE THEM A GOOD FIGHT TO FIGHT.** GIVE THEM A JOINT "ENEMY" (LIKE WORLD HUNGER OR POVERTY). ALLOW THEM TO BOND AS A TEAM.
>
> THIS MEASURE ALONE WILL GIVE YOU IN MANY CASES A **PRODUCTIVITY BOOST OF MORE THAN 50 PERCENT** OR EVEN 100 PERCENT. **THIS IS REAL MONEY THAT IS COMPARATIVELY EASY TO GET.**

You need to be clear on "why" your company exists. What ills does it fight? Why should your employees care? This purpose or mission statement, or, as I call it, a "why statement," is critical in driving your company to its full potential. In the table below, I am giving you a few hints on how to write an effective "why" statement.

Checklist: Create an Effective "Why" Statement for Your Company

- ✓ **Address a "big" topic or problem:** Small topics do not have "pull power." If you want your team to get out of bed early and excited, if you want them to put in extra effort at work, then you have to link your "why" statement to a big topic (like fighting poverty, world hunger, or diseases). Your employees need to feel that their work has meaning and makes a difference in the world.
- ✓ **Emotional:** You need to charge up your "why" statement emotionally. Link it to people as opposed to just making money (e.g., "…improving the lives of millions by…"). Look in people's eyes when you read the draft version to them. If they light up, you know that you are on to something.
- ✓ **Give people a fight:** Use strong and emotionally charged words like "fight" (as opposed to weak words like "improve").
- ✓ **Crisp and understandable:** Your "why" statement needs to be understandable to all employees, potential customers, and other stakeholders. Use simple language, short sentences, and no jargon.
- ✓ **Visually everywhere:** Put your purpose or "why" statement in the entrance/reception area and conference rooms. Your team needs to "breathe it."
- ✓ **Live it:** Anchor the purpose or "why" statement in your day-to-day life. For example, when making a decision, ask yourself whether this contributes to getting one step closer to achieving your purpose.

Yes, 99 percent of companies have purpose or mission statements, but most of them are of little use because they have no teeth. They are too general, too abstract, with no emotion, and too long. Let's look at the purpose/mission statement of SpaceX (the company founded and run by Tesla CEO Elon Musk) as an example of a good "why" statement:

> *"SpaceX designs, manufactures, and launches advanced rockets and spacecraft. The company was founded in 2002 to revolutionize space technology, with the ultimate goal of enabling people to live on other planets."*

The first sentence briefly describes WHAT the company does. The second sentence touches on WHY the company exists (what their PURPOSE is). It states a noble goal (enabling people to live on other planets) that many people can emotionally relate to.

MOVING TO ACTION: QUESTIONS TO ASK YOURSELF

- ✓ Why does your company exist? What good fight are you fighting? What is your "enemy?"
- ✓ What could a good "why" statement look like for your company?
- ✓ Does it emotionally touch your employees and customers? Is it brief and understandable? Is it quotable?

20. Set the Bar High

"Shoot for the moon. Even if you miss, you'll land among the stars."

— Norman Vincent Peale

Steve Jobs knew it. Elon Musk of Tesla and SpaceX knows it too. Many of the great sports coaches know it. The key to achieving outstanding results (the Apple iPhone, the Tesla Roadster, a Super Bowl win) is to set a super-ambitious target for your team and make them believe that they can achieve it. That's it.

Let me illustrate the difference between a normal target and a super-ambitious target. A normal target is to drive up sales by 5 percent or maybe 10 percent versus last year. Or to reduce production costs by 3 to 5 percent. These are small, incremental targets; they can be reached by continuing to use your existing processes and just working a little harder and smarter. They hardly get your team to question the status quo, and they rarely get them inspired.

A super-ambitious target, on the other hand, is to "put a man on the moon by the end of the decade" or to "develop an intuitive, interactive phone/music player/browser within the next three years" or to "build a car that sells for less than $5,000."

These goals challenge your team to find new and innovative ways because the current practices would never allow them to reach the goal. These goals can inspire your people to work long hours. These goals get your teams out of their comfort zones. And when they reach these goals, they will tell their grandchildren about it 50 years from now.

> ## 10x RESULTS "MILLION $ IDEA"
>
> ONE OF YOUR MOST IMPORTANT JOBS AS A CEO, OWNER, OR MANAGER IS TO ALWAYS CHALLENGE YOUR TEAM TO DO THINGS **MUCH** FASTER, **MUCH** BETTER, **MUCH** CHEAPER, OR SELL AT A **MUCH** HIGHER PRICE.
>
> ASK: **WHAT WOULD IT TAKE** TO PRODUCE AT HALF THE COST, TO GET THE PRODUCT TO MARKET IN HALF THE TIME, TO REDUCE FAILURE RATES BY 98 PERCENT, TO SELL AT A 50 PERCENT PREMIUM?
>
> **MASSIVELY CHALLENGING TARGETS GET YOUR TEAM TO LOOK AT NON-CONVENTIONAL WAYS OF DOING THINGS,** AND THIS WILL ULTIMATELY GET YOU MASSIVE RESULTS.

So, the next time you sit down with your team to discuss the sales targets for next year, don't discuss whether sales projections should go up by 5 percent or 10 percent. Instead ask them: "What would it take to double sales within the next three years?" Asking this question will likely get you one of the best team discussions that you've had in a long time.

Your people will take their gloves off and ponder questions like: "Should we change our pricing model, (e.g., to pay-per-month)? Should we partner with a large retail chain to leverage their distribution network? Should we enter the Southeast Asian market? Should we re-brand one of our products? Should we offer additional services that complement our core products? Should we move to a hunter and farmer sales model?"

In the end, you may pursue only some of the ideas that were put on the table during the discussion, and this is okay. What is important is to have this discussion and challenge your team to take their blinders off.

There are a few simple rules that will help you to set effective, super-ambitious goals:

CHECKLIST: EFFECTIVE GOAL SETTING

- ✓ **The 25 to 50 percent rule of thumb:** Aim for 50 percent more than what your first instinct tells you. For example, when you believe that a sales increase of 10 percent for next year is realistic, aim for at least 15 percent. When you believe that it will take your people three months to prepare the business case for an important project, aim for two months instead. Pressure will force your team to focus on what is really important and what really drives value.
- ✓ **Ask "what would it take?"** Always introduce these targets with the phrase "what would it take?" For example, ask your team "What would it take to grow revenues by 15 percent next year? What would we have to do differently? What are ideas and practices that we can leverage?"
- ✓ **Ensure real buy-in:** Setting a super-ambitious goal typically means that your people initially question whether the goal is realistic. Remain calm and factually address their objections one at a time. This is the only way to get their buy-in. Use the "what would it take?" question to brainstorm ideas on how to achieve the goal together with your team. This co-creation process will also increase their buy-in to the goal.

This brings us to the topic of how to get buy-in and how to best deal with objections. Invariably, when you set ambitious goals, you will get responses like "this is not achievable," "this is completely unrealistic," or "are you out of your mind?" It is okay to get these responses. The important thing is how to deal with them. It is unproductive to start a discussion on the details of why this cannot be done. Do not go down this route; this will get everybody in a negative mental frame and will not lead to them buying into your target.

Instead, ask a simple question: "What would it take for us to achieve this target? What would we have to do?" Asking this question will lead to a much more productive discussion around, for example, which resources to bring to bear, how to prioritize the initiatives, how to overcome obstacles. At the end of this discussion, you may have to adjust your target a little bit downward, but this is okay since it will still be much higher than if you had not communicated an ambitious target in the first place.

But now you have a target that inspires your team, that they believe in, and that will allow you to exceed the earnings expectations of the markets.,

MOVING TO ACTION: QUESTIONS TO ASK YOURSELF

- ✓ What are three to five areas in your business where you believe that your people are locked in a rigid mindset (e.g., "we should never sell direct," "we will never be able to get the new business win rate above 20 percent," "we will never be able to produce at 10 percent lower costs")?
- ✓ For these areas, which target would be high enough to disrupt their current thinking and instead get them to think of new, innovative ways to address these topics? Invite your key people to a workshop and discuss those ideas. In this workshop use questions like "What would it take to …?"
- ✓ What are the one or two areas where you have sensed the greatest buy-in from your people during the workshop? Take these areas and implement the agreed-upon measures. The goal is to quickly create a showcase of how ambitious goal setting can allow you and your team to achieve outstanding results.

21. Hire and Keep Only A Players

"Steve Jobs has a saying that A players hire A players; B players hire C players; and C players hire D players. It doesn't take long to get to Z players. This trickle-down effect causes bozo explosions in companies."

— Guy Kawasaki

A great company is like a great sports team. To be world-class, you need world-class players in all positions. If your offense is great, but your defense is weak or merely average, then you will not get very far in the playoffs. It is like the chain that is only as strong as its weakest link; so are also sports teams, and so are business teams.

To make it more specific, each person in your executive team has to be smarter or better in their functional area than you are. And the same applies to them and their direct reports and so forth. Take one of the greatest European soccer teams of the past decade as an example: Real Madrid has won the Champions League four times in the last five years. And they won not just because of Cristiano Ronaldo. They won because they have some of the world's best players on all positions.

Why does this matter to you? The difference between sports teams that win championships and those that come in second or third is massive (in terms of TV deals, merchandising, advertising, etc.). And the same also applies in business. Look at the smartphone market. Apple is able to capture a huge part of the profits that are being made in this industry.

There is one important caveat, and that is team chemistry. When push comes to shove, excellent teamwork or team chemistry always trumps individual brilliance. Take world soccer again as an example.

Argentina and Portugal have Lionel Messi and Cristiano Ronaldo on their teams, who between them have won the World "Player of the Year" award for the last 10 years in a row. Yet, it was the German soccer team that won the 2014 World Cup in Brazil. And it was the French team that won the World Cup in 2018. What helped them win the World Cup is their teamwork; everyone had each other's back. It was not about showing individual brilliance on the field at the expense of the other players. It was supporting each other to ultimately win as a team.

So, how can you go about identifying A players? Let's start with a definition. By A players we do not mean rocket scientists or future Nobel Laureates. By A players, we mean people who (1) are able to deliver, (2) are passionate and have a positive "can do" attitude, (3) are resilient when the going gets tough, (4) have character, are ethical, and, last but not least, (5) are true team players. In the checklist below, you can find more details on each of those points.

CHECKLIST: CHARACTERISTICS OF AN A PLAYER

- ✓ **Able to deliver:** Focused/does not get distracted; understands what the issues are and what it takes to resolve them; reliably delivers high-quality output; can separate the important from the unimportant.
- ✓ **Attitude:** Positive, proactive, and "can do."
- ✓ **Resilient:** Does not "freeze" when confronted with problems, but actively works at resolving them, able to deal with stress in a calm and thoughtful manner; does not explode.
- ✓ **Character:** Ethical and reliable.
- ✓ **Team player:** Is able to work in a team; supports all members of the team in their development; delegates, praises successes, and reprimands if needed.

Hiring the wrong person is exceptionally costly. It doesn't just involve the cost of the hiring and onboarding process (headhunter, interviews, training, etc.). But it is even more so the cost on the job. An employee who is only half engaged and delivers only average work will cost you not just in terms of this employee's individual performance, but also in terms of the performance of everybody around him. Team morale will sink, you run the risk of alienating customers, and you set the bar very low for others on the team.

So, how should you go about hiring the right person? First, you should have a crystal-clear view of what you are looking for (functional knowledge, personality traits/character, managerial experience, etc.). Second, you need to have a firm view on which of these criteria are must-haves and which elements you are willing to compromise on. Personally, I typically hire for "will" and train for "skill," meaning that if push comes to shove, attitude is more important to me than technical expertise. As a rule of thumb, make sure in your hiring decisions that you, at the minimum, weigh these two dimensions equally.

In my professional life, I have been part of about 400 hiring decisions. Here are some statistics that may help you calibrate your hiring decisions and fine-tune your hiring process:

- Out of the candidates who applied for a job, only one or two out of 10 were invited to a job interview.
- Varying by role, candidates had to pass three to six interview rounds of 45 to 60 minutes each (with different interviewers so that we got a holistic, unbiased view on the candidate).
- The interview consisted of real-world case studies to test the candidate's expertise as well as résumé questions to understand the candidate's qualifications and motivation to apply for the job.

- A "no" in any of these interview rounds meant a "no" overall. On average, only one out of five candidates who went through the interview process got a job offer. But of those candidates who received a job offer, the acceptance rates were very high (greater than 80 percent).

Because of this highly selective process, we could be sure that we hired only A players (and that almost none of these candidates had to be fired later for underperformance). Now, I am not saying that this process is for every company in every situation. But it has served me exceptionally well throughout the years.

How do I manage performance and how should I go about firing B or C players? Over the past decades, I followed a straightforward and transparent process that is detailed in the following checklist.

CHECKLIST: MANAGE PERFORMANCE/DEAL WITH UNDERPERFORMANCE

- ✓ **Clearly communicate what you expect/what excellent performance looks like:** The mistake that many managers make is that they are fuzzy about what they expect from their direct reports. "What are the deliverables?" "What does excellent performance look like?" "How will success be measured?" These are the questions that you need to address with your employee in great detail in early conversations. To do this well, you need to have these questions first answered for yourself before you speak with your employee. Once your employee is clear on the expectations, you can also stop micromanaging. Your employee will be able to manage himself or herself to a very high degree.
- ✓ **Give constant and unfiltered feedback:** Don't save the

feedback for the annual or semiannual, formal performance review discussions. I use phrases like "great job" or "that was a shitty job" almost daily with each of my direct reports. Don't sugarcoat and don't hold back. The process should be: (1) voice your emotion ("shitty job"), (2) explain why the performance was not up to par ("the numbers did not add up, and we used old prices for the offer"), (3) explain what you expect going forward ("double-check the numbers and the data sources; have a second set of eyes look at it").

✓ **Be explicit on what does not work well and what the consequences will be if the performance does not get up to par:** You expect a lot from your employees, but you must also communicate that it is okay to make mistakes. However, it is not okay to make mistakes repeatedly or deliver poor performance repeatedly. My approach is that if the same mistake or poor performance happens a second time, I say something like this: "This was the second time now; you need to get this under control. We cannot afford to lose customers over this. Do the double-checking/have a second set of eyes/re-look at the document as a printout. I trust that you will be able to fix this. This is serious now; if you cannot get this fixed, then we need to move you out of this role."

✓ **Fire/demote:** If you have followed the steps mentioned above, then the last step of firing the employee or moving him into a different role should come naturally. It will also be no surprise to the employee since you have been honest and transparent throughout the process. The important thing is that if poor performance continues, you will indeed need to follow through. You will need to fire the person or move him to a more suitable position. Otherwise, no one will take you seriously, and mediocrity will start creeping in.

Again, remember: One of the most toxic things is to keep underperformers in the organization (especially in parked leadership roles). This will send a bad message and significantly demotivate your best performers. They will then also not do their best work, and this will start a downward spiral.

I want to close this chapter with two of the most typical concerns that people have when I advocate this approach: (1) "But we are growing and I cannot afford to lose anybody" and (2) "The market is very tight; we cannot find any good talent." My response is: You cannot grow based on a weak foundation. Only strong A players will allow you to achieve the growth that you aspire to. If you do not consistently manage this process—also when talent is tight—you will not be able to become a great company. And great companies attract great talent. A players attract A players.

MOVING TO ACTION: QUESTIONS TO ASK YOURSELF

- ✓ Looking at your leadership team and also at the next level in your organization, do you have A players in all positions?
- ✓ If not, what can you do today to get A players who deliver exceptional performance into all of these positions?
- ✓ Can you coach them? Do you need to replace them?
- ✓ How can you implement a culture of A players in your business? How do you ensure this during the hiring process? The performance review process? The promotion and exit process?

22. Put Your People into Growth Roles

> *"Ability is what you are capable of doing. Motivation determines what you do. Attitude determines how well you do it."*
>
> — Lou Holtz

10x Results "Million $ Idea"

Think back on your career. **What were the times when you learned the most?** What were the times when you felt most energized? What were the times when you made the most significant steps in your personal and professional development?

I suggest that those were very **likely the times when somebody put you into a growth role:** When you got promoted to a job that, at that time, was still a little too large for you; when you had to stretch, work longer hours, learn through failure. But **you learned, and you learned a lot. This is the power of putting people into growth roles.**

There is also a flip side to this. Let me tell you a personal story: One of my friends from high school was very good at soccer. At least so he and I thought. But our coach was of a different opinion. My friend hardly got to play in the decisive matches. Over time, this made him very unhappy, and his game worsened. Fortunately for him, we got a new coach two years later. He saw the talent in my friend and had him play in a key midfielder position. My friend took on the challenge and quickly developed into one of the best players in our league.

The Reality in Many Companies

There are two lessons that I learned from this experience: (1) people are naturally motived, but (2) can become demotivated very quickly by being put into a role that does not stretch them. Today, many large companies face this problem. A lot of young talent is lost because they are stuck in roles that do not allow them to develop and stretch to their fullest potential.

This is a vicious cycle. It typically starts with the company hardly growing. As a result, very few new leadership positions become available. And when they do become available, an established person with more tenure is usually placed in this role. Over time, this crowds out the young talent. They seek employment at other companies where they are given greater opportunities. And this talent drain limits the growth potential of the company. What a waste!

So, how can this problem be solved? Start by weeding out C players at all levels in your organization, especially in management. This helps free up leadership roles that you can fill with your key talent.

How to Promote

Once you have opened up leadership positions, the next challenge becomes how to best fill those positions. In other words, based on which criteria should you decide whom to promote? Most people start with technical expertise. In principle, this is okay. But the mistake that many people make is that they expect their candidates to already come with all the experience that is required for the role.

As an example, for a country CFO role, they expect that the candidate has held this role before, perhaps in a smaller country. Also, they hope that the candidate has been head of accounting or head of controlling before. So, to put this in numbers, many hiring managers set the bar for technical expertise very high, at a 90 to 95 percent level. In my opinion, this is way too high.

My rule of thumb is 60/40. The candidate should have proven technical experience in 60 percent of what the new job requires. The remaining 40 percent knowledge gap is offset through the team. This demands that the direct reports are experts in their fields. This way, they can compensate for the temporary knowledge gap in the manager. And at the same time, the team will also be given greater freedom since the manager is not tempted to micromanage. This setup can work perfectly, but it requires trust, teamwork, and good people skills.

The table below gives you a few dimensions to look at when trying to identify the right candidate.

CHECKLIST: CRITERIA TO HELP DECIDE WHETHER TO PROMOTE A PERSON OR NOT

- ✓ **Passion:** Does this person have a burning desire for the job? Will he or she burn the midnight oil to achieve in this area?
- ✓ **A player?** Is this person an A player? Is this promotion a natural step in the development path of this person? Does the new role allow the person to build new skills in critical and important areas?
- ✓ **60 percent expertise:** Does this person have significant, relevant expertise (the 60 percent), but also enough room left to still grow and learn (the remaining 40 percent)? The mistake that many hiring executives make is to look for close to 100

percent expertise levels. As a result, those candidates are not stretched in the role and get easily bored, which will lead them to underdeliver.

- ✓ **At least two years in the prior role?** Typically, it takes about three to nine months for any individual to settle in a new position and contribute in a meaningful and substantial way. Only after two to three years, is a person typically fully rounded in a role and ready for promotion to the next level. The two- to three-year timeframe also allows you to see whether this person actually delivered in his or her current position.

How to Manage the Risks of Promoting Talent into Growth Roles

Promoting your key talent into growth roles comes with risks. These risks are manageable if, and only if, they are carefully and actively managed. Here is how to do it: (1) In the first three to six months, ensure that you check in more frequently. (2) Clearly define the deliverables that you expect from this person. Spell out precisely what constitutes excellent performance and what constitutes poor performance. For example, hiding problems, not asking for help, not leveraging the expertise of the team would be very high on my "poor performance" list. (3) If you have not yet done so, assign a mentor to this person. The mentor does not necessarily need to have complete technical expertise, but he or she should have comprehensive managerial knowledge so that coaching is possible on how to best deal with leadership challenges that the newly promoted person will face.

Moving to Action: Questions to Ask Yourself

- ✓ Do you know your key talent? Do you manage their careers actively?
- ✓ Do you fear that you and your management colleagues have been overly cautious when thinking of promoting key talent into leadership roles? How can you change this going forward?
- ✓ How can you ensure that you create opportunities for your key talent by actively managing out your C players in managerial roles?

23. Delegate Authority and Hold People 100% Accountable

"If you want to do a few small things right, do them yourself. If you want to do great things and make a big impact, learn to delegate."
— John C. Maxwell

10x Results "Million $ Idea"

One of the most demotivating experiences that many people have early in their careers is to have a **boss who cannot let go and micromanages everything**. This behavior has devastating effects both for the employee and for the manager.

The employee will become more and more insecure and disengaged, not putting 100 percent of his energy into the job. The manager will not be able to get many things done, because she gets lost in the details. Ultimately, the lack of trust in the employee's ability to do the job will become a self-fulfilling prophecy. The employee will indeed underdeliver and soon part ways with the company.

10x Results: Multiply the Value of Your Business

> **Addressing this problem in your company will lead to a massive boost in productivity, employee morale, and employee retention.**

The reasons for micromanaging are often twofold: (1) Young managers, especially, do not yet have the experience to delegate effectively. (2) In some cases, managers set very high standards of excellence, standards that no employee is able to meet, so they compensate by micromanaging and doing everything themselves. These problems can be addressed by following a few principles on how to delegate effectively:

Checklist: How to Delegate Effectively

- ✓ **Define the guardrails:** Whenever you start a new working relationship with an employee, it is essential that you have an explicit discussion on how the two of you work best together. Establish principles along the lines of "no surprises," "whenever problems pop up, I need to know right away," "it is okay not to know everything—ask me and ask your colleagues." These guardrails will help you avoid negative surprises.
- ✓ **Be 100 percent clear on what outcome you expect:** Most often the problems start where managers say "prepare a report on …," "draft the contract for …," "get me the documents for …" They do so without being specific on (1) what the final deliverable is supposed to look like, (2) how they will judge whether the deliverable is good, and (3) why they need the deliverable and what they need it for. Unless the report or contract draft are standard, and the employee has done this many times over, the outcome will likely not meet the manager's expectations. So, the first step is to be 100 percent clear on how you want the end result to look like. Here are a

104

few questions that you should ask yourself to get this sorted out: (1) "What do I need this for? Why do I need it?" Answering these questions will help you provide relevant context to the deliverable. You need to provide this context information to the employee so that he or she can work effectively without your constant guidance. (2) "What do I want to achieve with this?" Answering this question will help you get to the criteria that you will use to determine whether the deliverable is excellent or not. Based on the previous point, tell the employee (1) what you need, (2) why you need it, and (3) how you will judge the quality of what you get. The mistake that many managers make is that they just mention the first point—what they need—to the employee and forget about the other two points. But the last two points are at least as important as the first. They provide much-needed context that will help the employee in the process of working on the deliverable. The employee will be able to make decisions on her own if she knows what the work is needed for and how good quality will be judged. This allows you to take a step back.

- ✓ **Define clear deadlines and check-in times for draft reviews and the final document:** Especially, the first few times you try your hands at this new process, make sure that you schedule at least two or three check-ins to review drafts of the output. This will allow you to provide guidance and course-correct if needed. Since you still have enough time until the deliverable is due, you also do not need to overreact and take matters into your own hands again. You can let the employee continue with her work and learn in the process. When you have run this check-in process a few times, and both you and the employee know exactly what to expect, you can reduce the number of these draft check-in meetings.
- ✓ **Give feedback both on the quality of the deliverable and the quality of the process:** It is especially important early in

your working relationship that you provide constant feedback to your employee on how he or she is doing. Whenever something is off, say it immediately and say it explicitly without sugarcoating anything. Your employees will appreciate your candor and clarity. Be specific about what is off and make sure to provide recommendations on how to improve.

Following these five points for effective delegation will have massive positive effects: (1) Your employees will be happy because they feel empowered and not micromanaged, (2) You will be happy because you can focus on more important topics and do not have to do everything yourself, and (3) Your family will be happy because you come home earlier and more relaxed.

One last point: With delegation comes accountability. Be explicit that you will hold your people 100 percent accountable for the quality of their work. If they deliver sloppy work, if they repeat mistakes over and over again, they need to be reprimanded. And if this does not work, they need to be moved out of the position or even the company. You cannot allow that delivering poor quality work becomes acceptable in your company.

MOVING TO ACTION: QUESTIONS TO ASK YOURSELF

- ✓ What are five specific areas where you can delegate more?
- ✓ How can you best initiate this process with your employees? How can you ensure that the principles for effective delegation are followed?
- ✓ How can you ensure that people are held 100 percent accountable?

24. Make Each Day Count

> *"If you have to eat two frogs, eat the ugliest one first. This is another way of saying that if you have two important tasks before you, start with the biggest, hardest, and most important task first."*
>
> — Brian Tracy

Some 10 years back, my typical workday used to look like this: 80 percent of my time was pre-scheduled with calls and meetings. The remainder was largely taken up by quick check-ins with my team members and colleagues to fight the fires that popped up over the course of the day. Every two to three minutes a new email arrived in my inbox and demanded immediate attention. Well past 9 p.m. I came home exhausted. And when my wife asked me what I accomplished during the day, there was not much to show for. I understand that most managers across the globe and across industries experience pretty much the same.

It reached a point for me when something had to change. Simply working longer or harder was not a solution anymore. I developed a simple checklist for myself that I refined over the years. It helped me to get MUCH more done each workday. Here it is:

Checklist: How to Make Each Day Count

- ✓ **Preplan each day:** Every evening before I leave the office, I pre-plan the next day. I ask myself questions like: "What are the most important deliverables? How do I ensure that I get them done? Which important meetings or calls do I have? How do I ensure they are successful? How do I best leverage my team for the tasks at hand?" The result is a simple list of the key deliverables and meetings for the day (see the table below). By the way, I also use the same process for larger time intervals (week, month, quarter, year, decade). It is simple but works wonders.

- ✓ **The three most important deliverables:** ALWAYS identify the three most important deliverables for the next day and ensure that you allow sufficient time in your schedule to get them done.
- ✓ **First things first:** I typically aim to get the most important task of my day done before everybody else starts their workday. Starting 1-2 hours early, around 5:30 a.m. (and then also going to bed one to two hours earlier), will give you a tremendous head start into the day. You will feel a sense of pride and accomplishment early in the day, and this wave of positive emotions will carry you through the remainder of the day.
- ✓ **Batch email processing:** Never check emails as they come in and never check emails first thing in the morning. This will destroy your productivity and get you off on the wrong foot for the day. Instead, schedule two time blocks of one hour each for email processing. I typically have the first email block after lunch (to counter fatigue) and the second block after dinner with my family, when the kids are in bed. This still allows you a fairly decent response time of less than six hours for most emails, while protecting your "golden hours" when you are most productive. One more thing: I use email filters and auto-formatting to help me identify the 30 most important emails of the day out of a sea of 200+ emails. If you do not yet use these functions, give them a try. They're productivity boosters.
- ✓ **No multitasking:** I do not do emails while on calls. Either the call is important enough for me to attend, and then I listen and contribute, or I do not attend and do other more im-

portant work. I also have all social media turned off during the workday. Countless studies prove that multitasking is hugely ineffective and detrimental to your health and mental power. Don't do it.

Below, you can find an example, of how I typically preplan my day. In the column to the right, I have all important meetings and calls listed. In the other columns, I list the most important deliverables structured by area of responsibility (so, in my case transformation, strategy, and customer service). The three key deliverables for the day—that would make the day a success—and the associated meetings and calls are bolded and in italics. Every Friday evening, I draft the plan for the coming week. And then, on the night before, I review and update the plan for the next day. I have now used this method for almost 10 years, and I consider this one of the reasons for my success.

Daily Plan for July 2: Key Deliverables, Meetings, and Calls

------------------Key Deliverables------------------			Key Meetings & Calls
Transformation Europe	Strategy Europe	Customer service Europe	
France escalation resolved Role book finalized Personnel escalation Spain resolved	*2018 priorities aligned with other Board members* Agenda for 2018 management conference drafted Value-added services strategy reviewed	*10 commandments for world-class customer service aligned* Net Promoter Score results for Europe countries reviewed/ escalated	*8-9:30a.m. Customer heat map call* 1-2 p.m. Shared service center transition call 2-2:30 p.m. Prep call for next Board meeting (agenda, priorities) *3-6 p.m. 2018 priorities and CS commandments alignment calls with other Board members*

The beauty of this approach is that it helps you focus on the most important deliverables and meetings. That way you can make sure you get them done over the course of the day.

> ## 10x Results "Million $ Idea"
>
> Here is the **golden rule** to 10x what you get accomplished in a day: **(1) Know what the three most important things are that you have to get done today, (2) Write them down, (3) NEVER go to bed before you have achieved them.**

The "golden rule" sounds very simple, but its power and impact cannot be overstated. First, it gives you 100 percent clarity on what is truly important and what is not. What you will find is that most of the meetings and calls and to-dos you have scheduled for the day are not truly important and can either be canceled or delegated. This frees up time for things that really move the needle.

Second, writing them down ensures a sense of commitment. It will be much harder to say, "I'll move this to tomorrow morning because I rather watch a movie tonight" when you have put your commitment in writing.

Third, making a habit of actually accomplishing your three most important deliverables for the day will make it easier for you to do the things that need to get done. It will also give you a very powerful motivational boost.

> ## 10x Results "Million $ Idea"
>
> Motivation is often misunderstood. In this regard, our brains follow a very simple rule: **Motivation comes by itself through daily visible progress toward a goal.** At the end of the day you need to feel that you have accomplished something important. Then you will also feel motivated to accomplish even greater things the next day.

When identifying the three most important deliverables, I use a very simple rule of thumb. I ask myself, **"Will achieving these deliverables allow me to reach my goals for the month in a very significant way?"** Let me illustrate this with an example: Let's assume you are an entrepreneur and your target for new business wins next month is $1 million. Ask yourself, what are BY FAR the three most important things that you can get done today to help you achieve this target? It may be that well-prepared prospecting call that lands you a pitch meeting with your ideal prospect. Or it may be the escalation meeting that you have with one of your current customers who threatens to pull their business. And by acing this meeting, you not only protect your current business but also win additional business. Or it may be the meeting with your sales team to ensure that they are fired up, hungry, and have the necessary skills to win big.

MOVING TO ACTION: QUESTIONS TO ASK YOURSELF

- ✓ What are the immediate steps that you can take to make your days much more effective (pre-planning, focusing on the three most important deliverables, starting early, email batch processing, etc.)?
- ✓ How can you teach your team to do the same?
- ✓ How can you ensure that everybody in your organization gets their three most important deliverables for the day accomplished, every day?

25. Deep Work

> *"Two core abilities for thriving in the New Economy:*
> *1. The ability to quickly master hard things. 2. The ability to produce at an elite level, in terms of both quality and speed."*
>
> — Cal Newport

Imagine the following situation: You are trying to finalize the presentation for an important client meeting tomorrow. If you succeed, this could result in a multimillion-dollar contract. The stakes are high.

Then, one of your team members pops into your office to ask for advice on how to best prep for an upcoming internal review meeting. Two minutes after your colleague leaves the office, you get an email from your CFO—he urgently needs the investors' presentation from last year. You spend 15 minutes looking for the document and send it. Then, you're back to your sales pitch for tomorrow. But five minutes into the work, you get a text from your spouse about an important dinner that you host on Saturday. And so the list goes on and on.

We increasingly spend our time hopping from one task to the next, and then back. This is very bad both for our body and for our productivity. Contrary to popular belief, we are not able to multitask. We single task but often switch between tasks in very short time intervals. This leads to shallow work and shows all the symptoms of extreme stress (higher pulse and blood pressure, exhaustion, irritation, etc.).

The remedy is to clear your calendar of less important meetings and calls (cancel or delegate attendance) and to instead block out uninterrupted time for yourself to do real, deep work. Here is how it works:

> ## 10x Results "Million $ Idea"
>
> **Block out a time window of 90 minutes each day** that you keep "sacred." Personally, I always try to schedule these 90 minutes in the mornings from 6:30 to 8 a.m. This way, I am able to protect them from the craziness of the normal workday.
>
> Then, **use these 90 minutes to work on the most important task of the day.** This could be to finalize your speech for the investors' conference, or to prep for the must-win customer pitch, or to prepare your speech for the upcoming town hall meeting where you will launch a major change initiative.
>
> Stick with this regime for at least three weeks. I can almost guarantee you that you will become addicted to these 90-minute time blocks, as you **start accomplishing much more in these 90 minutes than throughout the remainder of the day.**
>
> Personally, I try to have at least two of these 90-minute time windows each day—with **no interruptions (no phones, no people, no noise, and no email).**

To ensure that you have 90 minutes without interruptions, review the following checklist on how to create an environment for deep work.

Checklist: How to Create an Environment for Deep Work

- ✓ **Highest energy hours:** Schedule your 90-minute deep work sessions in time slots where you have the most energy for productive work. For me, this is the morning hours between 6 and 11 a.m. Find the window of time that best fits your biorhythm. Put the time slot into your calendar.
- ✓ **Non-peak hours:** I try to schedule my 90-minute deep work sessions either during early mornings or late evenings to protect them from the craze of the regular workday. For other people, the lunch hours from noon to 1:30 p.m. appear to work.
- ✓ **No distractions:** Eliminate all outside distractions. Tell your executive assistant that you are unavailable for calls or other interruptions. Put your phone in "do not disturb" or airplane mode. Turn off all instant messaging (IM) and social media on your phone and laptop.

10x Results "Million $ Idea"

For most senior executives and Board members, more than **90 percent of your day is typically pre-scheduled** with meetings and calls. As a result, the risk is that you are driven by events and not the other way around.

Really **get 90 minutes of "alone, thinking time" each day early in the morning.** You will soon notice that you will get much more accomplished throughout the

> DAY. THE INVESTMENT OF THESE 90 MINUTES PAYS OFF MULTIPLIED.
>
> YOU WILL NOTICE THAT **THIS IS THE TIME YOU NEED TO SET THE STRATEGIC AGENDA FOR YOUR COMPANY AND TO BOOST REVENUES, PROFITS, AND MARKET CAP.**

MOVING TO ACTION: QUESTIONS TO ASK YOURSELF

- ✓ How can you block out a time slot of 90 minutes per day for deep work? What other activities do you need to deprioritize?
- ✓ How can you ensure that you will not be interrupted during these 90 minutes?
- ✓ Once you experience the effectiveness and productivity boost that these 90 minutes give you, ask yourself: How can I role this out to my team?

26. Make Your Meetings and Calls 10x More Effective

> *"People who enjoy meetings should not be in charge of anything."*
>
> — Thomas Sowell

Meetings and calls can be two of the most effective and productive ways to get things done in any company. Why is it then that everyone complains about them, saying, "Waste of time," "I didn't even know what we were supposed to discuss," "Too many people on the call," or "All talk, no decision."

Below is a list of the most common reasons why meetings and calls go wrong.

Checklist: Most Common Mistakes that Lead to Ineffective Meetings and Calls

- ✓ **Too many people invited:** If the meeting is to discuss and decide on a topic, then 10 people is the max that you should go with. Invite only people who can really contribute to the discussion. Having too many people will derail the conversation as everybody feels the need to say something.
- ✓ **A key stakeholder or decision maker is missing:** Making a decision with one of the key stakeholders missing will typically lead to this person resenting the decision. This often leads to an otherwise perfectly good decision being "fought to the death" just to make a point.
- ✓ **No agenda and meeting objectives:** A meeting where it is

unclear what the expected outcome is (inform, discuss, decide) and where the topics that will be discussed are not known or communicated up front is ineffective. It will help you better prepare the meeting if you are clear on the meeting's objectives and agenda. It will also help all participants to better prepare for the discussion when they have this information. Put the meeting objectives and agenda in all meeting invites.

- ✓ **Too much time scheduled:** Most meetings and calls could easily be cut in half without any loss in discussion content and outcome. Scheduling meetings for too long will lead to them starting late, idle chitchat, and people wandering off topic.
- ✓ **Meeting begins 10 to 20 minutes late:** If you wait for all people to arrive, you indirectly tell them that it is okay to come late. This is a waste of time and impolite to the people who came on time. Don't do this. Educate people to be on time by starting on time.
- ✓ **Scheduling a meeting when a call would do:** Meetings involve more effort (travel time) and are more costly (travel, accommodations) than calls. Don't ask for a meeting unless you truly need one. Personally, I never have people fly in for a meeting that is less than half a day. Video-conference technology is now good enough—use it. The only exception is customer meetings. But even here, video-conference technology is becoming more and more accepted.
- ✓ **Scheduling a call when an email would do:** When your objective is to inform on a topic that is not contagious, and when a direct feedback loop is not needed, then don't schedule a call. Inform everybody by email or a post on the company's intranet.
- ✓ **No meeting minutes and no follow-up:** Meetings and calls without minutes and follow-up on the agreed actions are like the meeting never happened. Invest 10 minutes to write and send short, crisp meeting minutes (and a thank you). This will

save you two hours for a repeat of the discussion a few weeks down the line because you did not take the time to recap the actions and ensure follow-up.

You probably experience all of these problems with meetings and calls in your day-to-day business life. But it does not have to be this way. Again, the way to resolve these issues is not to do away with meetings and calls, but instead to follow a few simple rules to make your calls and meetings much more effective.

CHECKLIST: RULES FOR EFFECTIVE MEETINGS/CALLS

- ✓ **Cancel all meetings and calls unless absolutely needed:** If it is just to inform, can this be done in a better or equally effective way by email or a post on the intranet?
- ✓ **Focus calls and meetings on "discuss, align, and decide" topics, not "inform":** Use meetings and calls to discuss "hairy topics" and initiatives that really move the needle.
- ✓ **Always have a clearly stated objective and agenda:** What is the expected outcome of the call or meeting? What will be the three to five key questions or topics that will be discussed? Having clarity on these three to five points and communicating them in each meeting or call invite will at least double the effectiveness of these meetings/calls.
- ✓ **Shorten the meeting/call time by 25 percent:** Some people schedule 30-minute calls and one-hour meetings out of habit, when less time is actually needed. Don't do this. If a topic can be discussed in 10 minutes, then schedule a 10-minute call. Again, this is to educate people and not waste everybody's time. If you schedule the call for 30 minutes, then it will take 30 minutes. But a significant part of the call will be spent either waiting for people to dial in or discussing off topics.
- ✓ **Start and finish on time:** Start on time to educate people to

be on time. Finish on time to be mindful of everybody's time and other commitments. If needed, schedule a follow-up discussion, but don't have meetings run over.
- ✓ **Summarize the decisions and action points:** Send meeting minutes out on the same day (at the latest, the next day). Plus, follow up on ALL agreed action items and decisions.

10x Results "Million $ Idea"

MEETINGS AND CALLS WITH **(1) CLEAR, WRITTEN OBJECTIVES, (2) A CLEAR, WRITTEN AGENDA, (3) THE RIGHT PEOPLE INVITED, (4) A SHORT ENOUGH TIME BUDGET TO KEEP PEOPLE FOCUSED, AND (5) MINUTES AND FOLLOW-UP ON AGREED ACTION ITEMS** ARE SOME OF THE MOST EFFECTIVE MEANS TO GET THINGS DONE IN ANY COMPANY.

MOVING TO ACTION: QUESTIONS TO ASK YOURSELF

- ✓ Looking at your calendar for this week and next week, ask yourself: "Can any of these meetings and calls be either canceled or shortened?"
- ✓ Do all calls and meetings have clear objectives and a clear agenda? Are the right people invited? Is everybody well prepared so that a decision can be made at the meeting?
- ✓ Are the actions from all calls and meetings followed up on consistently? If not, how can you ensure this going forward?

27. Money Is Not Everything— Publicly Recognize and Praise Excellent Performance

> *"Praise the slightest improvement and praise every improvement. That inspires the other person to keep on improving. [...] Be hearty in your approbation and lavish in your praise."*
>
> — Dale Carnegie

I have a request: Reach out to your 10 best performing people and ask them a simple question, "What are the top five reasons you work at our company and deliver such excellent performance?" You may be surprised by some of the answers you get. Responses may include:

- *"My work is meaningful. I feel that I can have a real impact in the world."*
- *"My colleagues are great people—smart, funny, do not take themselves too seriously. They help me to become better every day."*
- *"I feel valued by my coworkers and managers—both as a person and as a functional expert."*
- *"My compensation package is competitive."*

What you will likely find is that money and overall compensation will never make the top of their lists (in some cases it may not even be among the top five). What you will also find is that it is sometimes the little things that make a huge difference in employee engagement, performance, and happiness: The company off-site meeting at a beautiful location, the well-deserved praise from the boss in front of coworkers, the small, but meaningful Christmas present, the boat rafting tour with coworkers, or the barbecue party at the boss's home.

I like to think of it this way: Competitive compensation may be the entry ticket to get A players on the bus, but it is the other factors that keep them on the bus and keep them performing at exceptional levels.

What does all of this mean for you? My experience is that if you want to get and retain a team of A players, you should pay slightly above industry average, but well below industry max. As an example: Let's assume that the industry average for one of your department head positions is $150,000 base salary with a $50,000 target bonus. The industry max would be $200,000 base and $75,000 target bonus. My recommendation would be that you keep the base salary at industry average level ($150,000), but move the target bonus closer to the max level ($75,000). Ensure that the target bonus is linked to KPIs that the employee can genuinely influence and that would constitute great performance in this position.

A players are motivated by a challenge. They will readily accept this challenge and excel. In the end, you may have to pay out even a bit above the target bonus level, but you will get MUCH more value in return. Not just financially, but also in motivation, performance, and bottom-line results.

Only B and C players will go for a higher base and lower bonus component; this is also a good acid test to tell whether someone is an A player or not. But you do not want to have B and C players on the bus anyway.

> ## 10x Results "Million $ Idea"
>
> **Give constant (and by this, I mean <u>daily, almost hourly</u>) feedback to your people.** This can be one- or two-sentence feedback like: "Excellent how you handled the client's objection on the call" or "Bob, this was really a shitty job; there were errors on every page of the document, and you confused the client with our jargon during the presentation. I know that you can do much better. Show me your best in our next client meeting."
>
> I am not a friend of holding back feedback or sandwiching bad feedback. **Give feedback timely, in plain, direct language, and with specific examples.**
>
> If you make a habit of doing this, then: **(1) You will see rapid improvement in the performance of your people, (2) You will see their motivation go up, (3) You will not surprise them during performance reviews, and (4) Over time, you will be able to manage them less**, because they know what constitutes excellent performance.
>
> The cardinal rule of feedback applies: Positive feedback/praise in public; negative feedback in private.

Having said this, there are three specific points to remember when giving feedback:

Checklist: Double Your People's Performance Through Effective Feedback

- ✓ **Do it daily (almost hourly):** Whenever you notice good or bad performance, comment on it directly. Praise will boost their motivation at the moment and for the rest of the day. Reprimanding will as well if the feedback is (1) justified, (2) specific, and (3) contains specific and realistic action steps to improve.
- ✓ **Use plain, direct language:** Don't beat around the bush. If the performance was shitty, say so. It is okay if the person sees that you are disappointed.
- ✓ **Provide clear action steps on how to improve:** Your team needs to have a crystal-clear understanding of what constitutes excellent performance and what precisely they need to do to get there.

I have one more insight for you: Look at the military. Many of our young soldiers go through great sacrifices and risk their lives. In no small part, many of them do this to ultimately be awarded a bronze or silver star or even a medal of honor. I am not saying that our men and women in uniform do this only for the award. It is undoubtedly mainly to support their fellow servicemen and servicewomen and because duty calls for it. But the medals and public recognition play a significant role.

You can use the same psychology in your company as well. Create a system of medals, badges, and awards that inspire people to strive for excellent performance. Make sure that the system is built in such a way that 80 percent of your people have a good chance of winning the entry-level award. Twenty percent should be able to win the second-highest award. And the 5 percent top performers should be able to win the highest award. Create a theme around these awards similar to the military (e.g., "For superb customer service," "For a great innovative idea that will boost our bottom line"). I am sure you will come up with better names that inspire your team and reflect your company values. Do it. Do it now. You will be surprised at how your productivity and employee engagement will skyrocket.

Again, here is a quick summary of the main points:

CHECKLIST: OTHER IDEAS (THAT COST YOU ALMOST NOTHING) TO BOOST THE MOTIVATION AND PERFORMANCE OF YOUR TEAM

- ✓ **Medals, badges, awards, etc.:** Not just in insurance sales, medals, badges, and awards are an excellent way to publicly recognize your people and drive exceptional performance. Whoever gets the award is motivated and who does not get the award will be even more motivated to get it next time. This is the secret to excellence in professional sports; winning the championship trophy drives teams to go many extra miles.
- ✓ **Employee or team of the month or week:** Same reasons as for the above. Put their picture in a public place where everyone can see it, physically and on the intranet. Ideally, put next to it the three to five reasons this person or team received the award (so that everybody else knows what they need to do to win it too).

Moving to Action: Questions to Ask Yourself

- ✓ What award/medal system can you put in place to motivate your people to give it their best effort? What should the medals be awarded for? What names would you give them? Be sure to follow the more detailed recommendations above.
- ✓ How can you use positive feedback and active coaching to increase your team's motivation and commitment to go the extra mile (beyond the money)? Think of great sports coaches; how can you model your behavior after them?

28. Manage by Deliverables, Not Tasks

> *"Unless commitment is made, there are only promises and hopes; but no plans."*
> — Peter Drucker

Have you ever been in this situation? You give a task to one of your direct reports. Shortly before the deadline, you get what you ask for—so you think. But then you have a look at it and realize that this is not really what you had in mind. It is actually quite far off. After three more iterations and working into the late evening hours, you finally have something that is about 80 percent of what you initially had in mind.

Sounds familiar? Then you also know what the consequences of this situation are: (1) You had to invest a lot of your time, which came on top of everything that you had to do that day. (2) You and your employee are both fed up and demotivated. (3) You fear that the next time you ask for something, you will have a repeat of the same situation.

There is a much better way that saves you time, saves you and your employee frustration, and gets you much better results. And this is managing your team by deliverables, not tasks.

What is the difference between the two? While a task is merely an activity, a deliverable is an end result. It is something concrete like a signed contract, a completed excellent annual report, or a produced winning marketing commercial. It is an outcome that is spot-on, that clearly meets what you had in mind.

Let me illustrate this with one example: Let's assume you have an important meeting with a prospect a week from now. You have invested a lot of your personal time over the past three months to get this meeting and, if successful, a multimillion-dollar contract could be the result of it. So how do you ensure that the meeting document that you ask your employee to prepare is top-notch/fit for this purpose and will help you win the contract? Here is the checklist to help you achieve just that:

Checklist: What Makes a Powerful Deliverable

- ✓ **Explain the why:** Top prospect; a lot of money on the line; winning this would make our numbers for the year (and bonuses).
- ✓ **Provide lots of context:** What problem is the prospect trying to solve? What are the hot buttons? What competition are we up against? What is our unique selling proposition? How much time do we have for the meeting? How will the document be used in the discussion? How can we stress our key points of differentiation? What are no-gos for the prospect (errors, small font, color blind, etc.)?
- ✓ **How will you evaluate whether the deliverable is excellent?** Makes a compelling case that the prospect needs to take action. Makes a compelling case that we are by far the best provider. Is crisp, short, with plain and powerful language, and convincing charts and graphics. Speaks to the emotional side.

10x Results "Million $ Idea"

The extra 15 to 30 minutes invested up front to provide rich context and explain what an excellent deliverable would look like will save you and your em-

> PLOYEE COUNTLESS HOURS IN REWORKING A SUB-PAR DRAFT. **YOU WILL GET AN EXCELLENT FIRST DRAFT THAT JUST NEEDS SOME FINAL POLISHING.** YOU WILL BE HAPPY; YOUR EMPLOYEE WILL BE HAPPY, AND MOST IMPORTANTLY, YOUR PROSPECT WILL BE HAPPY WHEN YOUR PRESENTATION IS RIGHT ON TARGET (AND YOU SIGN THE DEAL).

Other Benefits of Managing via Deliverables

Motivation comes from the daily visible progress toward a goal. When your employees know exactly what the expected final deliverable should look like, and when they feel like they have made good progress toward that end deliverable throughout the day, they will also feel energized and motivated. This motivation comes from within the employee; there is nothing more that you need to do.

There is one other benefit. Often, an excellent deliverable can be created in many different ways. What is important is the outcome, not how the employee got there. By communicating what end result you expect (the deliverable) and leaving how to get there (the tasks) largely up to the employee, you will free yourself from having to micromanage the employee. And in the process, you will even boost the motivation of your employee.

CHECKLIST: EXAMPLES OF GOOD DELIVERABLES

- ✓ **Pitch presentation:** "We need to win this contract. We need to sweep them off their feet. The presentation needs to relate to their most pressing pain points and build a bridge to our proposed solution. In the end, it needs to be crystal clear that (1) they need to take action, (2) that we have the perfect solution, and (3) that we are the perfect partner for them and can deliver."

- ✓ **Marketing commercial:** "We need to win with the 20-something segment. We need to get into their heads and think like they think (Instagram, YouTube, and Snapchat). We need to appeal to them. They need to truly believe that our brand is the coolest and that they MUST have our product as THE "it piece" of the season."
- ✓ **All-hands call with the team:** "We have 30 minutes for the call. I want to leave the last 10 minutes for Q&A. In the call, we need to celebrate our recent successes. The employees need to come out super-motivated and fired up. We also need to explain why we drive the "excellence in everything we do" initiative. Let's give them the three best reasons this is important and what they can do in their day-to-day work to make it happen."

MOVING TO ACTION: QUESTIONS TO ASK YOURSELF

- ✓ Look at the meetings that you will have today and tomorrow: How can you phrase the tasks that you want to give to your team more as deliverables?
- ✓ How can you give them better context on (1) why this deliverable is needed, (2) what it will be used for, and (3) what constitutes excellent work?

29. Keep Your People's Energy Levels High

> *"We survive on too little sleep, wolf down fast foods on the run, fuel up with coffee and cool down with alcohol and sleeping pills. Faced with relentless demands at work, we become short-tempered and easily distracted. We return home from long days at work feeling exhausted and often experience our families not as a source of joy and renewal, but as one more demand in an already overburdened life."*
> — Jim Loehr, Tony Schwartz

My Wake-Up Call

It was a Friday morning about five years ago. I was in my doctor's office for a regular health check-up: blood screening, respiratory function tests, electrocardiography, skin check, weight/BMI, blood pressure.

Then, the doctor called me in to discuss the results. My blood pressure was at a critical level, LDL cholesterol was above average, BMI was borderline, and my overall cardio fitness was well below that of my peers. The message was simple: I had to do something, or I could expect a stroke or heart attack within the next 10 to 15 years.

At work, I had always been proud that I was the person who could go the extra mile: Work a little longer, produce a little more, sleep a little less. Coffee kept me going—often more than 10 cups a day. Not to mention the Coke and fast food for lunch. This had to stop.

The Reality in Many Companies

Unfortunately, my story is not the exception, but rather the norm in many companies. This is costing people valuable months and years of their lives and costing companies billions in decreased work productivity and increased sick leaves.

When much of the workforce comes to work in the morning on too little sleep and no breakfast (or unhealthy breakfast), then you can already predict how the day will go. This has to change.

Over the last 10 to 15 years, many companies in the U.S. and around the world, have recognized the problem and are trying to counter it with company health programs: Fitness studio memberships, fruit baskets, Fitbit watches, and yoga classes. All of this is very good. But for it to bear fruit, the program needs to be followed consistently.

10x Results "Million $ Idea"

You cannot force people to eat healthily, sleep well, and exercise regularly. Mandated company health programs, therefore, need to be complemented with an element of peer pressure. **"Positive peer pressure" is the key. When your colleagues go out for a short walk over lunch or eat fresh veggies and fruits throughout the day** (instead of that candy bar and Diet Coke), **then you are much more likely to do the same.** Take one step at a time; no large, big bang initiative, but **a bit more (sleep, healthy eating, and exercise) every day.**

What We Can Do about It

On the following pages, you can find short checklists that may give you some ideas on where to start. Again, do NOT try to do it all at once. Instead, try to add one more item from these lists to your daily routine each week. After half a year, you will see that most of these items will have become daily habits that you (and your people) do naturally. Don't force it—go step by step.

Something to consider: While the ideas below will work for 99 percent of people, you may be the exception. So, consult with your physician before starting the program, as I am not a physician and, therefore, cannot give medical advice.

CHECKLIST: EAT AND DRINK FOR PERFORMANCE

- ✓ **Water:** Drink half a gallon (two liters) of water or herbal tea a day. Your brain needs hydration to function well. I like unsweetened herbal or fruit tea, since they are not as dull as plain water and add essential minerals to the body. Unsweetened lemon water also works.
- ✓ **Eat fresh vegetables five times per day:** I always take fresh bell peppers, carrots, avocados, and cucumbers with me to the office. Whenever I feel the first signs of hunger, I have those, plus some nuts and an apple.
- ✓ **Cut sugar and refined products:** You get enough sugar from the regular food you eat; there's no need to add more sugar. Eat products in their natural state (e.g., meat), not heavily processed (e.g., as sausages or spread).
- ✓ **Enjoy your food, eat slowly:** This will help you avoid overeating and improve digestion.
- ✓ **Eat fatty fish** (like salmon) three times a week for the omega-3 fatty acids.
- ✓ **Coffee/black tea:** Have a max of three cups of coffee or

black tea a day. Ideally, have herbal and fruit tea instead. I have cut my coffee intake from 10 cups to two cups a day (one for breakfast and one after lunch) and feel more energized than ever.

- ✓ **Alcohol—a max of two glasses of red wine, a max of three times per week:** If you must have alcohol, keep it to a max of two glasses of red wine (which many studies have proven has health benefits). Try to have as little hard liquor and beer as possible.
- ✓ **Eat whole-fat products:** Regular butter and milk are better for your body than skimmed versions. Mix this with salads (with olive oil) and you will soon notice that you can eat less and still feel well fed.
- ✓ **Quality over quantity:** Go for good-quality, organic food that is as close to its natural state as possible (meat, dairy, veggies, fruits). Often frozen veggies and fruits contain more vitamins since they are frozen directly after harvest than so-called fresh foods that have been transported for days or even weeks (unless you get them directly from the farmer).

CHECKLIST: INCREASE YOUR FITNESS LEVEL

- ✓ **At least five minutes of walking/standing time each hour:** Much of our back pain and other health issues can be relieved with five minutes of walking each hour. This improves your posture and reduces tension in your muscles. Do your phone calls while walking; have one-on-ones with your people while walking outside (this also gets you some vitamin D from the sun).
- ✓ **Get at least 20 minutes of physical exercise each day:** Do whatever you like best. For me, this is bodyweight training twice a week (e.g., when I am on the road, in a hotel room), Taekwondo classes twice a week, running 10 miles once a

week, and stretching/Pilates/yoga twice a week. Alternate the training and allow a bit of time for warm-up/stretching and cooling down. Pick a time that works best for you and stick to it. For me this is evenings, but many people do it first thing in the morning.
- ✓ **Body fat below 20 percent:** Get a scale that measures body fat and aim to get it to somewhere south of 20 percent. BMI is not a good measure since it does not differentiate between body fat and muscles.
- ✓ **If possible, get a Fitbit or Apple Watch (or similar device):** Get a fitness-tracking device. Here, the mantra "what gets measured gets managed" really applies. Seeing your statistics evolve from one day to the next gives you a tremendous motivational boost to further improve. I significantly lowered my weight and improved my physical fitness the first six months after I got my device.
- ✓ **Regular health check-ups:** Get your blood and urine tested at least once every two years. Ideally, also include an ECG, respiratory checks, and diagnostic sonography. Measure your heart rate and blood pressure regularly.

CHECKLIST: GET EXCELLENT SLEEP

- ✓ **Aim for at least seven hours of uninterrupted sleep:** Yes, some people may need less, but for more than 90 percent of us, seven hours of sleep is what we need at minimum. This equals about 7.5 hours in bed if you count the time you need to fall asleep and the time you wake up throughout the night.
- ✓ **10 p.m. to 5:30 a.m.:** Stabilize your biorhythm by sticking to regular bedtimes and wake-up times (ideally maintain the rhythm also on weekends). Go to bed early (this way you avoid overeating on chips or popcorn, and drinking too much Coke and alcohol) and get out of bed early (ideally 5 a.m.) to

get a head start into the day.
- ✓ **20-minute "cool down" before lights out:** No emails, phone calls, or computers. Instead, read a book, meditate, or talk to your spouse.
- ✓ **Cool:** Aim to have the room at 65°F/18°C.
- ✓ **Dark:** Lower the shades and put all electrical devices with monitors away.
- ✓ **Fresh air:** Open the windows before you go to bed. If you need to keep them closed at night due to outside noise, then at least open the door to the adjacent room for enough fresh air throughout the night.
- ✓ **No electronic devices in or near your bed:** Put your cell phone at least three feet away from the bed.
- ✓ **Do not disturb:** Turn your phones to "do not disturb/silent mode."
- ✓ **Set two alarm clocks (for 5 a.m.):** Set two alarm clocks with soft, ascending ringtones (in case one alarm does not go off).
- ✓ **No snooze button:** Get out of bed when the alarm rings. Hitting the snooze button is one of the worst things that you can do for your body/your vitality. You will feel tired throughout the day.

MOVING TO ACTION: QUESTIONS TO ASK YOURSELF

- ✓ From the lists above, what are two daily practices that you will start doing to improve your physical fitness? Your eating and drinking habits? Your sleep?
- ✓ How can you create this mindset of healthy living in your company? Discuss ideas with your management team. Perhaps also ask two or three more junior people; often, they will have terrific ideas.

30. Summary: Key Insights and Action Plan

Use these two pages to capture the thoughts, epiphanies, revenue and profit ideas that came to your head when reading the last couple of chapters. Take 20 minutes to jot down the ideas. You will find that this time is very well invested. We will refer to this summary at the end of the book.

Book Section: "Multiply the Productivity of Your People"—My Action Plan

- ✓ Epiphanies/aha moments from this section: ……………
  ……………………………………………………………………
  ……………………………………………………………………
  ……………………………………………………………………
  ……………………………………………………………………
  ……………………………………………………………………
  ……………………………………………………………………
  ……………………………………………………………………
  ……………………………………………………………………
  ……………………………………………………………………

- ✓ What I will immediately start implementing with my team as of next Monday morning: ……………………………
  ……………………………………………………………………

....
....
....
....
....
....
....
....
....
....

- ✓ **Game-changing ideas that require thought and careful preparation. Assign a Board member to prepare a proposal on how to best implement/capture max benefits:** ....
....
....
....
....
....
....
....
....
....
....
....

DRIVE INNOVATION AND GROWTH

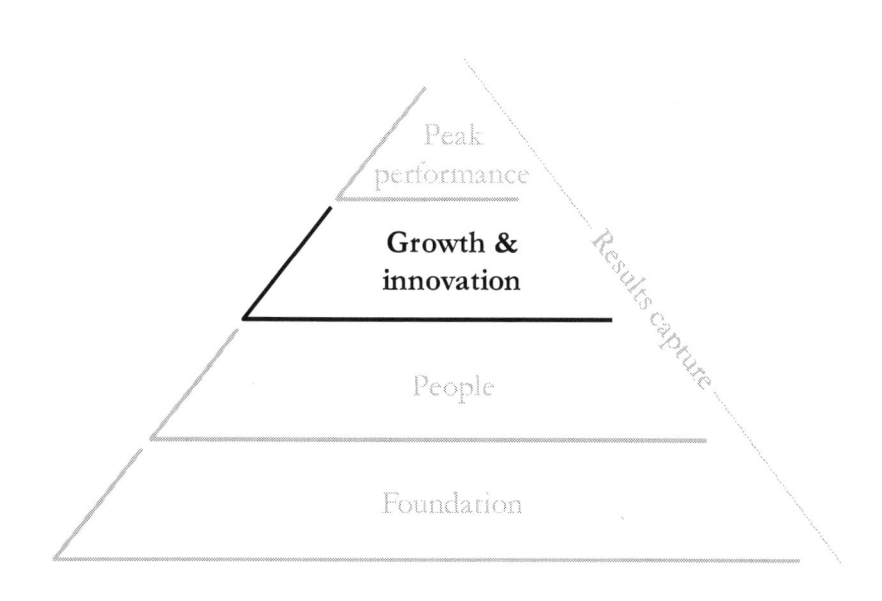

31. A Powerful Framework for Business Growth

> *"The key to sustained and profitable growth is to find a repeatable formula that utilizes the most powerful and differentiated strengths in your core and applies them to a series of new 'adjacent' markets."*
>
> — Chris Zook

Unfortunately, many companies go about business growth the wrong way. Here is what typically happens: Revenues are flat for a few quarters. Then, (almost) every opportunity for business growth is pursued—entering a foreign market, opening up a new business line, joint ventures, and so on. But, unfortunately, a few quarters down the line, revenues have not only remained flat, but now also profits have taken a significant hit due to the investments in the pursued growth opportunities. There is a better way.

10x RESULTS "MILLION $ IDEA"

RULES ONE, TWO, AND THREE OF BUSINESS GROWTH ARE TO FIRST FIX YOUR CORE BUSINESS AND BRING IT TO FULL POTENTIAL BEFORE GOING AFTER MORE DISTANT GROWTH OPPORTUNITIES.

IF YOUR CORE BUSINESS IS WEAK—PROCESSES ARE BROKEN, PRODUCT QUALITY IS TERRIBLE, MARKETING AND SALES PRODUCTIVITY ARE WEAK, INNOVATION PIPELINE IS DRY—THEN THIS IS WHERE TO START. **FIX THESE AREAS, TURN YOUR CORE BUSI-**

> NESS AROUND, AND THEN YOU WILL SEE PROFITABLE GROWTH FROM IT. YOU WILL BE SURPRISED AT HOW MUCH THERE IS TO FIX IN YOUR CORE BUSINESS AND HOW SIGNIFICANT THE BENEFITS ARE FROM FIXING IT. ONCE YOU HAVE DONE THIS, YOU CAN—FROM THIS POSITION OF STRENGTH—GO AFTER OTHER OPPORTUNITIES.
>
> AS A RULE OF THUMB: **IT TYPICALLY TAKES AT LEAST TWO TO FOUR YEARS TO GET YOUR CORE BUSINESS TO FULL POTENTIAL. DURING THIS PERIOD, FOCUS ON YOUR CORE BUSINESS AND STOP CHASING EVERY RABBIT THAT SHOWS UP.**

CHECKLIST: HOW TO BRING YOUR CORE BUSINESS TO FULL POTENTIAL

- ✓ **Fix product/service quality issues:** Understanding the root causes of product failures and service breakdowns should be the first step in any improvement effort. The reason is simple: Excellent product and service quality will lead to customer satisfaction and loyalty, which in turn leads to repeat purchases and recommendations of your products and services to friends and other associates. Hence, your business will grow.
- ✓ **Improve your sales and marketing prowess:** Once, you have fixed the product and service issues, the next step is to ensure that your products and services are positioned as well as possible in the market. What is your unique selling proposition? How can you make sure that this message gets through to customers? Do your salespeople have all the training and tools they need to sell well? Are the incentives aligned? Does your marketing message position you as the go-to provider for your service?
- ✓ **Optimize and streamline your business processes:** After

you have tackled the above two points (which ideally should not take more than six months), the next step is to get your processes to world class. Can you streamline the processes? Can you automate them using IT? Can you reduce process failures? Can you cut down process time?

✓ **Build innovation pipeline:** Last, but not least, make sure that your products and services stay fresh and relevant. Ensure that your innovation pipeline is full. Do not just look internally. Also, see what innovations from other companies you can bring to bear.

How do you know that your core business is at full potential? Here are a few hints: (1) You get excellent customer feedback (measured by Net Promoter Score or another customer metric), and a significant share of your new business volume is generated by customer referrals. (2) Your profit margins are among the best in your industry. (3) You have a very low (and still decreasing) number of customer product or service failures. In short, your processes are under control.

When you have exhausted the growth opportunities in your core business, you can start looking for growth opportunities elsewhere. But where do you look?

10x Results "Million $ Idea"

In the business world, we can draw excellent lessons from the world of sports: **A world-class athlete in the 100 meter competition can also become world class in the 200 meter or the 4x100 meter relay. But this person will never become world class at fencing** or even at the 5,000 meter distance. The capabilities to win at these disciplines are just too different.

Drive Innovation and Growth

> NOW TAKING THIS BACK TO THE WORLD OF BUSINESS, **WHEN YOU WANT TO PRIORITIZE GROWTH OPPORTUNITIES OUTSIDE YOUR CORE BUSINESS, ASK YOURSELF: "IN WHICH OF THESE AREAS CAN I BRING MY CORE STRENGTHS BEST TO BEAR AND WIN?"**

Typically, these are areas that are relatively close to your core business. The checklist below lists some of the most typical adjacent growth areas:

CHECKLIST: WHERE TO FIND NEW GROWTH

- ✓ **New geographic market:** One of the first steps typically taken when you have exhausted the growth potential in your home markets is to enter new countries—be it Europe, Asia, Latin America, or Africa. One of the best strategies is to sync up this geographic expansion with your key customers. Follow them when they enter a new market, but only after you have done your homework and determined for yourself that this market indeed has tremendous potential for you. This will allow you to hit the ground running.
- ✓ **New product (variants):** Let's say you are a brewer. Your beer is good, but consumption is not growing anymore. But you see that the market for specialty beers (Corona, mixed/spiced beers) is growing. Entering this market, you can still leverage most of your current strengths.
- ✓ **New customer segments:** Adobe Premiere Pro or Adobe Photoshop CC are primarily solutions for professionals, but Adobe also targets the consumer segment with the somewhat skimmed down versions of Adobe Premiere/Photoshop Elements.
- ✓ **New sales channel:** Many companies who offer more so-

phisticated products and services have now recently started to also sell those services online. Other examples are companies that have begun to build their own direct sales teams where historically they relied on third parties.
- ✓ **New services:** Last, but not least, you can also offer additional services that go with your primary product. Some car manufacturers now turn in a higher profit with after sales and spare parts than with their core "selling automobiles" business.

To summarize: First, fix your core business. Then, from a position of strength, go into related fields where you can leverage most of your world-class capabilities.

MOVING TO ACTION: QUESTIONS TO ASK YOURSELF

- ✓ Where are the most significant pain points in your core business? What is your action plan to fix them over the coming 12 to 24 months? Which Board member takes the lead on each of these individual initiatives? How do we track progress and hold everybody accountable?
- ✓ In which areas is your company world class (or can be)? To give you two examples, this could be capabilities like developing highly innovative energy storage solutions or building close and trusted relationships with healthcare professionals. The next question is: In which additional nearby markets can you leverage these strengths?

32. The Best Business Growth Engine: Customer Referrals and Testimonials

> *"People influence people. Nothing influences people more than a recommendation from a trusted friend. A trusted referral influences people more than the best broadcast message. A trusted referral is the Holy Grail of advertising."*
>
> — Mark Zuckerberg

Let's do a quick back-of-the-envelope calculation. How much money do you spend in acquiring a new customer? Perhaps, you do print, radio, and TV advertising. Maybe, you have an in-house sales team to generate leads. Perhaps, you have a field sales team that visits the customer an average of five times before a sale is made. Plus travel time. Plus dinners. That is a lot of money spent. For many companies, new customer acquisition costs can easily go into the hundreds, thousands, or even tens of thousands of dollars per new customer.

10x Results "Million $ Idea"

Most companies **vastly underutilize the power of customer referrals and testimonials.** They remain passive—when a referral happens it is great—but it is not actively managed.

> **PEOPLE TRUST THEIR FRIENDS AND COLLEAGUES MUCH MORE THAN SOMEONE WHO THEY BARELY KNOW.** So, why fight windmills when you can use current and past customers to power the windmill for you?
>
> You need to **MANAGE REFERRALS MORE SYSTEMATICALLY**: When signing a new customer, you need to tell her that your goal is to provide exceptional service so that she will go back to her colleagues and friends and recommend you to them. This sets the scene and also the service promise.
>
> Then, **ONCE YOU HAVE DELIVERED EXCELLENT SERVICE (AND ONLY THEN), YOU HAVE EARNED THE RIGHT TO ASK FOR A REFERRAL OR TESTIMONIAL.** And in nine cases out of 10, you will get it because you have set the expectation up front.

The two checklists below can help you get started to manage your customer referrals and testimonials to a much greater degree. Since sales to businesses and sales to private individuals need to be treated somewhat differently, I have put them in two separate checklists:

CHECKLIST: BUSINESS SALES—POWERFUL REFERRAL AND TESTIMONIAL IDEAS

- ✓ **Testimonial videos and quotes:** After a successful project, ask the customer CEO for 15 minutes of her time to shoot a testimonial video (ensure good lighting, sound, and setting). Prepare three to four high-impact questions that allow your customer to praise you ("delivered, knowledgeable, excellent customer focus, good people to deal with, will use again"). From the answers, it has to become clear that the CEO is a true fan of your work. Have the video professionally edited for max impact (lower thirds, cutting, intro/outro, music, three to five minutes max). Use key quotes from the video for selling presentations and on your website. Have the CEO sign off on the final video and quotes.

✓ **In high-stakes sales, take your best clients (current or past) with you to meetings with potential clients:** I suggest that you do this not at the first meeting, but at the second or third meeting when you aim to close the deal. To do this, offer to bring a current client with you (or video conference him or her in) in your first meeting. It is very powerful to have a customer speak on your behalf. The customer can praise you much more than you could do yourself.

✓ **Discuss potential referrals:** Toward the end of your engagement, ask the client for a 30-minute meeting. Say something like: "Bob, I want to ask you for your help. Thanks for telling me that you are very pleased with the work that we are doing for you. We would also like to support some of your friends and their companies. Perhaps there are a few names that come to your mind. Could we have your ideas on which challenges they face and how we could potentially support them? Thanks Bob!" Most clients will be happy to support you (and their friends). It's a win-win. You just have to have the courage to ask for it.

CHECKLIST: CONSUMER SALES—POWERFUL REFERRAL AND TESTIMONIAL IDEAS

✓ **Customer testimonials:** Make it super-easy for customers to leave a testimonial on your website. Ideally, first ask the NPS question ("How likely is it that you would recommend our

company/product/service to a friend or colleague?"), and for promoters, follow that up with a request for a short testimonial. For detractors, get in contact with them to see whether you can turn around the customer experience.
- ✓ **One-click email or web form referrals:** After you have provided exceptional service, ask the customer (once you have validated that she is indeed super-happy) to recommend your product or service to three friends. Make it specific. Ask for more than one recommendation. And make it easy; send an email with a link to an easy-to-fill web form to put in the prospect names and a personal two-liner for introduction. It should not take your customer more than two minutes for three introductions.

One final thought: There will be times when potential customers are referred to you, but you ultimately cannot help them. Perhaps your product or service just does not fit what the customer needs. It is okay and honest to say so up front. But the next step is critical: Try to refer this potential customer to another business colleague who can service this customer better. Doing so will be a big favor to both the potential customer and the business colleague. Typically, they do not forget; and you will see the favor returned to you multiplied.

MOVING TO ACTION: QUESTIONS TO ASK YOURSELF

- ✓ What do your ideal customers look like? Who has access to them (business associates, professional associations, school, church)? What is the best way to ask them for a referral?
- ✓ How can you manage referrals and testimonials more systematically? When do you ask your customer for a referral or testimonial? What are the prerequisites? How exactly do you do it? Do you do something in return?

33. Punch Above Your Weight: Joint Ventures and Partnerships

> *"Yet the case for collaboration is stronger than ever. It takes so much money to develop new products and to penetrate new markets that few companies can go it alone in every situation."*
>
> — Gary Hamel, C. K. Prahalad

About 10 years ago, Tom and Bob teamed up to start a tax consultancy in Germany. Business went well; they grew the company to about 20 professionals. But for the last two to three years, business remained flat. This was mostly due to the increased margin pressure in their core business: National tax declarations for mid-size companies. Tom and Bob decided to start offering tax services for international clients on cross-border taxation issues. They put their eye on Dubai as the first market to enter. Cross-border tax advisory is a much more lucrative business, but harder to get in (especially as a small, local German tax consultancy).

So, what did Bob and Tom do? They decided to team up with a mid-size, local tax consultancy in Dubai. Over the past couple of years, a lot of German companies entered the Dubai market and now need advice on how to optimize taxes. By themselves, the German and the Dubai tax consultancies could not offer this service. But together they can. Business is brilliant.

Then, Tom and Bob took the next step. They noticed that many companies wanted to get integrated tax and legal advice. Again, by themselves, they could not play in this market. So, they teamed up with a law firm. Together they can now provide integrated services without cannibalizing each other's core business. So, what is the lesson?

10x Results "Million $ Idea"

Independent of whether you are running a **small startup or a multibillion-dollar corporation, you can greatly benefit from leveraging other companies assets for your own purposes.** If structured well, this is a clear win-win for both companies.

Here is how to start: Together with your management team, **identify two to three great product or service areas that are vastly underleveraged today.** Identify what is holding you back: Are you lacking access to a key customer segment? Are you lacking access to a key distribution channel? Are you lacking access to state-of-the-art production facilities to produce at scale and low cost?

Find companies that have precisely these capabilities (ideally from outside your industry so that you do not directly compete with them).

Understand what you could offer them to make it worth their while. Then go and take action. Playing by the rules that everybody follows in your industry will not get you anywhere. **Be the innovator. Be the rule-breaker.**

When identifying areas for potential partnerships or joint ventures, three spheres need to be looked at:

> ### CHECKLIST: HOW TO START AND WHAT TO LOOK AT
>
> - ✓ **The missing ingredient:** You have a great product or service, but a critical capability is missing to bring it to full potential. So does the other company.
> - ✓ **Win-win:** There is a clear case for a win-win between the partners. This is typically the case for companies from different industries that have complementary capabilities. In other words, joint ventures and partnerships between companies from the same industry often go south (due to rivalry, one company gets the upper hand, lack of trust).
> - ✓ **Explicit on the details:** It needs to be clearly spelled out up front what each party brings to the table, how the JV will be run and governed, how conflicts will be resolved, and how the profits will be split.

What worked for Bob and Tom can also work for you. Again, joint ventures and partnerships are a perfect way to grow for ambitious, smaller companies that lack critical assets. But even for large corporations, this can be a very attractive option. Whether you are the company CEO, the CEO of a business unit, or country CEO, there will be areas where teaming up with companies from other industries can help you propel your business to new levels of profitable growth.

Moving to Action: Questions to Ask Yourself

- ✓ Which two or three of your products or services could you grow exponentially if you had access to a critical capability that is missing today (e.g., access to distribution channel, access to a key customer segment, access to state-of-the-art production facilities)?
- ✓ Which companies (preferably from outside your industry) possess those critical capabilities? What could you offer them to make it worth their while? What is an offer they could not refuse?
- ✓ How would you structure the deal (governance, economics, day-to-day business, conflict resolution mechanism)?
- ✓ What is the best way to approach the other company?

34. Become World-Class in Winning New Business

> *"People don't like to be sold ... but they love to buy."*
> — Jeffrey Gitomer

What does it take to sell more? Is it learning the best closing techniques? Is it better prospect qualification? Is it better sales reporting and steering? Is it better sales training? Perhaps it's all of the above, to a degree. But this will only get you so far. There is an essential ingredient that still needs to be added:

10x Results "Million $ Idea"

Buying is highly emotional. We buy from people we TRUST and LIKE. Building this TRUST (in you as a person, in your company, in your products and services) **and this LIKING** (through increasing the level of similarity between the prospect and you) **are the keys to success in selling.**

It is as simple as that. So, then the natural follow-up question is: How you can increase the level of trust and liking between you and your potential customer? Glad you asked:

CHECKLIST: HOW TO BUILD TRUST AND IMPROVE THE DEGREE OF LIKING

- ✓ **Always do what you say (or promise):** Being someone who your customer can rely on is of utmost importance. Ultimately, your customer puts his career in your hands by asking you to help him solve one of his toughest problems. When you let him down, then trust is lost forever. So, don't do it. Always deliver. Always do what you say (or promise). Never promise what you cannot deliver.
- ✓ **Put your customer before yourself:** You are here to help the customer. That should be your priority number one, two, and three. Never put your own interests first. Potential customers will realize this very quickly and walk away (and rightfully so). Nobody wants to be in the hands of someone who takes care of his own interests first.
- ✓ **Be seen as the clear expert:** If your customer plans to hire you and your company, then she needs to trust that you actually have the expertise necessary to get the job done. How often have you done this successfully in the past? Can you prove it (i.e., with testimonials or professional training certificates)? Leave absolutely no doubt that you are indeed THE expert.
- ✓ **Make customers like you:** It is straightforward that we generally like people who are similar to us—come from the same town, went to the same schools, eat the same food, like the same sports team, dress the same way, talk the same way. Look for at least three or four things that you and the potential customer have in common. Are you both dog lovers? Do you both have teenage children? Did you grow up in the same neighborhood? Do you drive the same vintage car? Great. Share those stories. You will see both of your eyes light up as the emotional bond develops.

I believe that I cannot overstress this: Mastering the four points from the list above will already get you 80 percent of the way to sales success. They seem simple, but please take the time to read and re-read them, think about them, and put them into action. You will be amazed by the results.

The next step is a bit more tactical. How do you get the most out of every sales meeting and sales call? The following checklist will help your salespeople with this.

Checklist: Questions to Ask Yourself Before Every Prospect Meeting or Call

- ✓ **Objective:** What do I want to achieve with this call or meeting? What is the ideal outcome? ("Get the prospect to say yes to a trial? Get a meeting with the real decision maker? Get additional information to be able to better tailor the proposal?")
- ✓ **Prospect objections:** What are the objections that I expect from the prospect? What makes it hard for them to buy? ("Don't know us." "Happy with existing provider." "Price too high." "No time."). Be prepared to address those concerns directly.
- ✓ **Two or three "armor-piercing" arguments:** What are my two or three best arguments on why the customer should move forward with us? Avoid preparing too many arguments; focus on the two or three most important and rehearse the delivery.
- ✓ **Why now?** Prepare two "armor-piercing" reasons why the prospect needs to act now. A compelling case on the "why now" question is what many sales professionals forget and then ask themselves why they did not make the sale.
- ✓ **Make it easy to buy:** Make it easy for customers to buy when they are ready to buy. Have the contract draft ready. Offer a money-back guarantee or a trial.

The last element in achieving world-class status in winning new business is to become world-class in your formal final sales pitches. This is where many sales professionals still get it wrong. They prepare the PowerPoint slides until late into the night and then underwhelm the prospect with their oral presentation. Below are six action points that will help you significantly improve your win rate.

10x Results "Million $ Idea"

Whether you are successful with your pitch is determined 80 percent by HOW you present and only 20 percent by WHAT you present.

Here are a few simple tips that will increase your odds of winning exponentially:

(1) **Cut down the number of PowerPoint slides** at least by half.

(2) **Research who you will be talking to and relate to them on a personal level** early on in the presentation.

(3) Make the pitch into a **dialogue**. Allow for questions and address them right away. This keeps interest and attention high. Prepare dialogue triggers.

(4) **Rehearse your pitch presentation at least three times**. Get professional help if needed. Come across as professional, yet relatable. Be engaging and smile—relate to the people across the table.

> (5) **Know your three "armor-piercing" selling arguments and repeat them at least three times** each during the presentation and Q&A. Repeating them will help your potential customer remember.
>
> (6) Keep it simple and exciting. One of your most important jobs is to **keep your counterpart attentive and engaged.**

Moving to Action: Questions to Ask Yourself

- ✓ What is the best way to ensure that every salesperson knows and applies the "trust" and "liking" principles in their day-to-day job? How can you cascade this to the sales frontline staff?
- ✓ How can you make sure that the principles for effective sales calls and meetings are applied in each and every sales call and meeting—without exception?
- ✓ How can you implement the six principles for perfect pitches in every sales pitch going forward? How can you train your salespeople to do this? How can you coach them on the job?

35. Implement a World-Class Pricing Model

"Price is what you pay. Value is what you get."
— Warren Buffett

For many companies, this may well be one of the most important chapters of this book. First off, let's clear a few pricing myths.

Checklist: Pricing Myths and the Reality

- ✓ **"When you increase prices, volume will always go down:"** In many situations, this statement is not true. Customers see price as an indicator of quality. If the current price of your product is, in the eyes of the customer, very low for this type of product, then they equate this with low quality and don't buy. For example, if you are in the business of selling umbrellas, you may actually sell more umbrellas at a price of $20 than at a price of $5. This is because customers may believe that a $5 umbrella will break after the second use. So they rather go for the higher-priced version, expecting that it will last longer.
- ✓ **"The lowest price always wins:"** Even in many RFQ situations, it is rarely the lowest price offer that wins. Your price needs to be within an acceptable range, and then other factors become decisive. Does the client trust that you can deliver? Do you have a stellar track record? Of what perceived quality is your product or service?

- ✓ **"100 percent price transparency:"** With price comparison sites now everywhere, especially in the consumer segment, some people believe that it becomes ever harder to make a sale if your product is priced significantly higher than the competition. This does not have to be the case, especially if you unbundle price components. To illustrate, consider this example: You sell printers. They typically sell for $100, including the cartridge. If you unbundle ($70 for the printer and $30 for the cartridge), your printer will end up at the top of the list on all comparison sites. And likely you will still make the $100 sale since people will ultimately want their printers with cartridges.
- ✓ **"Only limited potential to innovate:"** Many companies are saying that they cannot deviate from the pricing model that is prevalent in their industries. I ask: "Why is that?" Even if you are not among the top three players in your industry, you still have the possibility to innovate. A good example is mobile phone plans. Some companies, like T-Mobile or O2, have been very successful with innovative pricing models.
- ✓ **"Price thresholds:"** This is a myth that actually works; pricing a product at $9.98 yields significantly higher sales than pricing it at $10. So, use them.

10X RESULTS "MILLION $ IDEA"

SET PRICES TO MAXIMIZE PROFITS, NOT REVENUE, NOT MARKET SHARE, NOT VOLUME, OR ANY OTHER MEASURE. TYPICALLY, THE PRICES THAT WOULD MAX OUT REVENUE ARE SIGNIFICANTLY LOWER THAN THOSE THAT MAX OUT PROFITS. BUT AT THE END OF THE DAY, PROFITS ARE WHAT COUNT, NOT REVENUE.

> **THE PROBLEM IS THAT MANY SALESPEOPLE ARE INCENTIVIZED BASED ON REVENUES.** TRY TO SUBSTITUTE THIS WITH A PROFIT COMPONENT (IF YOU DON'T HAVE ACTUALS, THEN USE CALCULATED PROFIT).
>
> SECONDLY, IT IS ESSENTIAL TO MAINTAIN A LONG-TERM VIEW. STRUCTURE THE PRICING IN A WAY SO YOU CAN EXPECT REPEAT PURCHASES (AT LOWER CUSTOMER-ACQUISITION COSTS). **IT IS THE LIFETIME (PROFIT) VALUE OF A CUSTOMER THAT COUNTS,** NOT WHATEVER PROFITS YOU CAN MAKE TODAY.

Some people argue that Amazon used a market share-based pricing model for a very long time and that this is what made Amazon successful. They say that Amazon showed losses for a very long time, but at the same time tremendous revenue and market share growth, and now the company reaps the benefits.

My response? Yes, in certain situations it makes sense to first drive market share so that you can command a price premium once you have a dominant market position. But, first, you may very quickly find yourself in an anti-trust situation. And, secondly, this strategy requires significant investment and patience. Only very few companies and investment funds will, therefore, be able to go this route.

Finding the right pricing strategy is always context specific: It depends on which industry you're in, your positioning (premium versus value), and your growth ambitions. Therefore, this book can only give you a few hints on which strategies work in most industries.

CHECKLIST: THE PRICING BASICS

- ✓ **Trials to build confidence:** Often, potential customers are hesitant to buy because they do not yet know whether the product or service will deliver on what it promises. You can

overcome this hesitance by offering the customer a limited-time trial at no or low cost.
- ✓ **The trust factor:** Beyond trials, there are other ways to build trust in your product or service. Celebrity endorsements still work since the trust that they have earned reflects on you. A money-back guarantee typically also works since it reflects your confidence in your product or service being able to deliver.
- ✓ **When in doubt, go premium:** Today, it is tough to pull off a price leadership strategy. It requires significant investment to be able to produce the products or services at such a low cost and still return a profit. You need to be a clear market leader (or at least a close second) to achieve solid profitability levels. If there is no way for you to get there in the nearer future, then price leadership is not a good strategy for you.

CHECKLIST: A FEW INNOVATIVE PRICING STRATEGIES THAT WORK

- ✓ **Loyalty program:** Loyalty programs can be an excellent way to tip the scale in your favor. For example, look at airline loyalty programs: Many people go to great lengths to get their flights booked on their favorite airlines to maintain or elevate their program status. Loyalty programs can be combined with volume incentives (e.g., discounts when reaching a specific purchase volume) and value incentives (e.g., free airline lounge access or hotel room upgrades). Try to find an incentive that does not cost you much in addition, but offers enormous added value to the customer (e.g., room upgrades in hotels).
- ✓ **Freemium:** Used a lot, for example, for internet services. You have an attractive basic offer that is free. The primary goal is to tie in the customers, then once the customers have tasted

your product, you move them to a premium version. Many apps on the Apple App Store and Google Play work this way.
- ✓ **Auction and reverse auction:** If you have privileged access to a sought-after product (e.g., art, valuables, prime real estate), the best way to sell it at a max premium would be an auction model.
- ✓ **Intelligent surcharges:** Many price comparison sites take whatever price you also show on your website. Sometimes, it is a wise idea to unbundle your product, so that it shows up as one of the top offers on any product comparison site. You can then still provide additional services and products.
- ✓ **Paying in installments combined with a money-back guarantee on the first installment:** In some instances (i.e., when customers first need to try a product before they can appreciate its full value) it may make sense to offer payment in installments combined with a money-back guarantee for the first installment, in case the customer is not happy.

10x Results "Million $ Idea"

The **psychology of pricing**: Price is seen as an indicator of quality; high price equals high quality.

If you **combine a high list price with a significant discount** (e.g., north of 10 percent), then many customers believe that they get an excellent product at a very attractive price. If you **make this offer expire within a few days or mention that it is valid for the first 1,000 purchases only, then you get customers to take action**. (Creating scarcity works wonders.)

> AN ALTERNATIVE TO AN ACTUAL PRICE DISCOUNT WOULD BE **ADD-ON SERVICES AT NO EXTRA COST**. THE BENEFIT OF THIS STRATEGY IS THAT YOU ACHIEVE HIGHER REVENUE AND SHARE-OF-WALLET (AT THE SAME PROFITABILITY LEVELS).

A closing statement: Price discipline generally increases a company's market valuation. What this means for you is that before you start cutting prices, make sure that you have looked at all other ways to act (i.e., bundling, unbundling, change of price scheme, brand push, celebrity endorsement).

MOVING TO ACTION: QUESTIONS TO ASK YOURSELF

- ✓ Assuming that repeat customers are the most profitable, is your current pricing scheme targeted to acquire precisely those customers?
- ✓ Are your pricing strategy and your product/quality promise aligned?
- ✓ How can you use some of the pricing strategies that are mentioned in this chapter?
- ✓ Do you see ways to adjust the pricing scheme to get higher profits and share of wallet from your customers?

36. Take Calculated Risks

> *"Only those who play win. Only those who risk win. History favors risk-takers. Forgets the timid. Everything else is commentary."*
>
> — Iveta Cherneva

Evolution has taught us to be a bit more cautious: Don't attack the animal if the risk that you get eaten is very high. From an evolutionary perspective this is probably a good thing. After all, we humans are still living on planet Earth.

However, in today's modern life, there are relatively few life-or-death situations. Getting rejected by a potential date is not; switching jobs is not; starting your own business is not. Overall, many situations in our day-to-day life are far less dangerous than our prehistoric brains make them out to be.

Let's assume you are contemplating the idea of selling your products and services in foreign countries. You are quite successful in the U.S., but have no experience abroad. How would you enter the market? How high is the potential risk of failure (i.e., stiff competition, limited access to key distribution channels, weak institutions/red tape)? How can these risks be mitigated? Could you partner with a strong local player? Could you launch a low-risk test pilot in one city? Could you use alternative distribution channels? Could you turn some of your disadvantages into advantages?

What you will likely find after you have pondered some of these questions is that the actual worst-case scenario risk is much lower than you initially thought.

> ## 10x Results "Million $ Idea"
>
> In many cases, **the "worst-case risk" of any strategic move** (i.e., sell a new product, enter a new market, use a new distribution channel, change marketing strategy) **is much lower than what we initially think.**
>
> Therefore, **whenever the next opportunity presents itself to you, don't say no right away.** Instead, write down what key risks you see and what potential mitigation strategies you could envision. Then, validate these with some of your key associates and experts on this topic.
>
> What you will get is **a much more balanced assessment** of the risks and opportunities, and what you will see is that **you end up saying yes to many more opportunities that will ultimately also show financially in strong top- and bottom-line growth.**

If we work from the assumption that many opportunities are actually worth taking, then the next question is how to better understand and manage the risks.

Checklist: Understand the Economics and Manage the Risks

- ✓ **Build a high-level model:** I always found it very helpful to build a high-level business model in Excel. If this is not your forte, have one of your experts do it for you. This gives you two main benefits: (1) You understand the economic drivers much better. This could be drivers like the number of customers, average purchase volume, economics per distribution channel, fixed versus variable cost blocks. (2) Understanding this allows you to improve the economics of the business case by posing and answering questions like: How can we lower the fixed cost block and convert it to variable costs? How can we drive up the average purchase volume? How can we incentivize purchases via our most profitable distribution channels?

- ✓ **Do sensitivity analysis:** The next step is to better understand how changes in each input variable will change the model output (typically NPV, IRR, profit cash flow projections). One of the best ways to do this is with "Monte Carlo" simulations. If you do not know how to do it yourself, have one of your data gurus do it. It will help you understand precisely how, i.e., changes in your pricing, volumes, or market conditions impact profits. It will assist you in developing strategies to deal with these risk factors effectively.

- ✓ **Understand the max downside and exit options:** If everything goes wrong, what is the max downside? Most people would say that losing all your investments is the max downside. But this is seldom the right answer. You could still sell the test business to a competitor who may be able to turn it around by integrating it with their processes. Or sell the parts to different buyers. Or use other risk hedging strategies.

Make sure that you include in your model macro trends that may impact the business case mid-term. Examples are changes in tax laws, expected new government regulations, technological trends, socioeconomic and demographic trends. Profit pools may shift due to these trends, and you want to be prepared when this happens.

CHECKLIST: HOW TO MANAGE RISKS ONCE YOU HAVE MADE THE DECISION

- ✓ **Milestones/gate reviews:** To understand whether you are still on track, you need to define clear milestones. For every milestone that you miss, you need to identify the root causes and define countermeasures. Also, I am a big fan of regular status reviews or "gate reviews" where you discuss where you are versus the initial plan. I typically have them once a quarter for longer projects, but it could also be as frequent as once a week.
- ✓ **Early warning indicators:** Identify lead indicators for potential trouble. This could be things like drops in the number of leads/prospects, win ratio, or spikes in customer attrition.
- ✓ **Hedge:** Hedging strategies include entering into a JV instead of going it alone or doing a smaller pilot first before going all in.

10X RESULTS "MILLION $ IDEA"

THE KEY TO SUCCESS IS TO **ENTER INTO A NUMBER OF SMALL BETS**—BUSINESS OPPORTUNITIES THAT HAVE SIGNIFICANT UPSIDE AND MANAGEABLE DOWNSIDE. IF ONE OF THOSE BETS GOES SOUTH, YOU MAY SEE A SMALL DIP IN PROFITABILITY, BUT YOU DO NOT STAND TO LOSE THE COMPANY.

ENTERING INTO THESE "SMALL BETS" ON BUSINESS OPPORTUNITIES **BUILDS YOUR "COMPANY MUSCLE" (OR CAPABILITIES) TO ENTER INTO RISKY SITUATIONS AND MANAGE THE RISK SUCCESSFULLY.**

MOVING TO ACTION: QUESTIONS TO ASK YOURSELF

- ✓ What are the 10 most significant business opportunities for your company? Brainstorm with your management team.
- ✓ What is the worst-case scenario for each of these opportunities? How can you manage/hedge the downside?
- ✓ What is the remaining risk? What is the upside from going for this opportunity (strengthened market position, top- and bottom-line boost)?
- ✓ Will you go for this opportunity (when looking at the remaining risk and reward profile)? Who on your team should drive this effort to success?

37. Double Down on Innovation

> *"Innovation distinguishes between a leader and a follower."*
>
> — Steve Jobs

What is innovation? Pause and think about this question for a moment. Most people, when they hear the word innovation, think about new products or new services. But innovation is so much more. It includes pricing innovation, product delivery innovation, supply chain innovation, sales and marketing innovation, and production innovation. So, next time when you have a discussion about innovation with your team, make sure that you look at all possible dimensions of innovation. Maybe it is not a product innovation, but a product delivery innovation that will propel your company to the next level.

10x Results "Million $ Idea"

When thinking about innovation, it is essential that you **switch your perspective**; do not look at products. Look instead at **(1) which customers do you want to serve, (2) what are their most significant pains/problems, and (3) how can your company's products and services help relieve their pains.**

Doing so will allow you to **envision novel products and services that cross the traditional product lines.** Look, for example, at the first Palm handheld

> COMPUTERS (THAT WERE DE FACTO ELECTRONIC FILOFAXES).
> NOW, COMPARE THIS TO THE FIRST IPHONE THAT BECAME THE
> FIRST REAL PERSONAL ELECTRONIC ASSISTANT (INCLUDING THE
> TRADITIONAL FILOFAX FUNCTIONS, BUT ALSO A CAMERA, PHONE,
> MUSIC, GAMES, APPS, AND MORE).

Now that we have established, that innovation is much more than just product and service innovation, I assume that your next question will be: "But where do I get great innovative ideas from?" Well, there are a number of excellent sources that you can tap into.

CHECKLIST: HOW TO GET NEW INNOVATION IDEAS

- ✓ **From customers:** Have structured interviews with your best and your most annoyed customers. If you are brave, you can also do this in a workshop setting (although I would not recommend starting with this). Brainstorm with them about the following questions: (1) What are some of the most significant pains or problems that you are facing today in your company or industry? (2) What ways do you see to resolve or at least ease those pains or problems? (3) What could our company do to help with this?
- ✓ **From competitors:** Legally gather competitive intelligence on the innovation pipeline of your competition. Study investor presentations, executive interviews, SEC filings, patent and trademark filings, recent acquisitions, job postings, and news clippings. All of this should give you an excellent feel for your competitors' plans.
- ✓ **From experts:** There are many consultants, academics, and other experts out there who have great ideas. You can get them from books, interview, and articles (e.g., *Harvard Business Review*). Make use of what is available.

- ✓ **From employees:** Create a forum to submit innovative product and service ideas. Make it fun; introduce a friendly competition in which an employee is picked once a quarter as the "innovation mastermind." In the table further below you can find more details on how to put this into practice.

So, how do you create a culture of innovation within your company? My firm belief is that innovation is not the job of a department within the company, but the responsibility of each and every employee. So your job is to create a culture and processes where innovative ideas are encouraged and valued, and where they are ultimately turned into great products and services for your current and new customers.

I am NOT an advocate of launching a big, new innovation initiative, but rather to grow this innovation culture and mindset organically. It may start as easy as this: In your next all-hands call with company employees, make a point along the lines of, "We as a company need to be more innovative to remain relevant to our customers and compete successfully. It will take all of us to do this; every idea from everyone is valued. It may just be what we need to propel us onto the next growth path. Therefore, we will give you an easy-to-use way to submit your innovation ideas. Each quarter, the three best ideas will be publicly recognized." The form that you use to capture the ideas could look like this:

CHECKLIST: "INNOVATION-ON-A-PAGE"

- ✓ **What is the innovative idea?** Brief two- to three-line description of the innovative idea. What is novel? In which area is the innovation?
- ✓ **What customer pain/issues does it address and resolve?** Ultimately, all innovations need to be tied back to help relieve a problem or pain that the customer has. Again, two to three

lines on what the customer pain is and how the innovation helps relieve it.
- ✓ **In which way is it better than anything else that exists today?** What is the crucial point of differentiation versus anything that is out there in the market? Is it cheaper, faster, better looking, more versatile? You name the key reasons.
- ✓ **How big is the (money) opportunity? A rough back-of-the-envelope business case.** For example: "Would help us win two million new customers who have a strong need for a solution like this, but at the moment do not buy because the current solution is way too pricey. Our solution is half the price of what is available today. And still we will generate a $5 profit per customer per year; that is $10 million gross profit per year. Net-net it is still around $8 million, after accounting for moderate cannibalization of our existing products."
- ✓ **What would it take to get it to prototype stage?** Five-person team (product design, production and marketing expertise) for six months, half a million in funding.
- ✓ **Categorization:** This is required so that you are able to categorize and prioritize the idea. For example: Product innovation, household appliances division. Use a drop-down list.
- ✓ **Who submitted?** Jack P. Parker, customer service team, Dallas.

Encourage submissions. Publicly praise the best submissions on a quarterly basis. Also, keep the innovation wheel spinning by bringing the first good innovation ideas to life quickly. Once your team sees that their ideas are valued and implemented, you will have a self-reinforcing virtuous process.

10x Results "Million $ Idea"

You are not just competing against your current competitors for your current customers. There is also typically a **vast segment of non-consumers**. These are people and companies that are currently not yet buying the products and services that you and your competitors are offering. This is a huge area of untapped potential.

Ask yourself the following questions: **(1) Why do these people/companies not yet buy our products and services? (2) Can we create a product or service that would better fit their needs (i.e., cheaper, other features, other pricing model, other marketing/selling)? (3) Is it worth going after this opportunity? And if yes, how?**

Moving to Action: Questions to Ask Yourself

- ✓ How can you tap into all sources for innovation (customers, competitors, experts, employees)?
- ✓ What is the best process to capture, prioritize, and manage those ideas?
- ✓ How do you ensure that innovative ideas are protected from "mothership bureaucracy" during the incubation stage? Do you need a different organizational setup?
- ✓ How can you tap into the potential of non-customers? What do you need? How could you serve them?

38. Put Your Growth on Steroids: Use Small-Scale Acquisitions to Close Capability Gaps

> *"Our business is really pretty simple. When you look at the deal and its structure looks like an octopus or a spider, just don't do it. That kept us out of a lot of things."*
> — Tim Sloan

Ask your top and middle managers one question: "Should we as a company do more M&A? Or less?" You will likely see that your team is split in half. Some people will fiercely argue against M&A, stating that it leads to the best people leaving, inward focus, and unrealized synergies. And then there will be people who will equally fiercely argue for M&A, stating that it helps the company build much-needed capabilities and expertise to win in today's market. So, who is right?

Both sides are right. If done wrong, M&A destroys company culture and shareholder value on a massive scale. But if done right, M&A can propel your growth to the next level. In this chapter, I will argue that you should probably do more M&A (of the right kind and for the right reasons).

What are some of the key learnings and insights around M&A that you can apply in your company right away?

Checklist: M&A Best Practices

- ✓ **Acquire significantly smaller companies:** There is no such thing as a merger of equals. When two companies of the same size merge, there will be massive infighting around positions and the prevailing company culture. It is much better to acquire significantly smaller companies (e.g., less than one-third of your size). Then, it is clear from day one who the acquirer is and who is being acquired. This will help ease and speed up the integration. Actually, in my experience, the best strategy is to do "micro-acquisitions" where the acquisition target has less than 5 percent of your revenues or number of employees. The primary reason to do these "micro-acquisitions" is to close important capability gaps. These "micro-acquisitions" have three main advantages: (1) They do not disrupt the company, (2) they allow you to "surgically" close capability gaps, and (3) they are very cost effective.

- ✓ **Acquire capabilities:** The principal reason for acquisitions should be to get a hold of capabilities that are a key ingredient to your future business success (proprietary processes, intellectual property, and/or products/prototypes). You should not acquire primarily for the people as they may leave relatively quickly. You should also not acquire primarily for cost synergy or market share reasons. These are very fragile due to potentially incompatible processes and a strong inward focus during the integration period.

- ✓ **Look beyond your industry:** Many companies look only within their industry for potential acquisition targets. In reality, often the most attractive acquisition targets are outside your industry. Remember, what you are after is unique capabilities that will allow you to provide exceptional products and services to your customers. You will not get this level of uniqueness when you only look within your industry.

- ✓ **Prepare well and do it quickly:** M&A is a period of enormous stress and pain for the organization. Minimize this painful period by pre-planning well (who to take on which job; where and how to integrate).
- ✓ **Decide on how to integrate:** Integration is not a black-or-white game (either full or no integration). Instead, be clear on where to integrate functions and processes and where to leave them separate.
- ✓ **Don't overpay:** Be clear on what the acquisition is worth to you (future earnings potential of the target plus synergies to your core business from transferred capabilities plus synergies from integrating selected processes). Discount the potential max acquisition price at least by 15 to 25 percent for difficulties that may arise during the integration, but are not yet foreseeable.

10X RESULTS "MILLION $ IDEA"

BUILD YOUR M&A MUSCLE. SUCCESSFULLY IDENTIFYING TARGETS, NEGOTIATING, STRUCTURING THE DEAL, INTEGRATING, REALIZING SYNERGIES IS AN ART THAT REQUIRES PRACTICE.

START SMALL; LEARN FROM IT AND THEN GRADUALLY BUILD YOUR M&A MUSCLE. NOT DOING ANY M&A IS AS WRONG AS GOING TOO BIG TOO SOON.

WHEN MAKING ACQUISITIONS, ALWAYS ASK YOURSELF: "WOULD THIS ACQUISITION ADD A CAPABILITY THAT IS CRITICAL TO OUR LONG-TERM SUCCESS? WOULD IT GIVE US A SIGNIFICANT ADVANTAGE VERSUS THE COMPETITION?"

The last question that remains is: "When should you acquire a company and when should you partner?" The short answer is: When the other company possesses a key capability or another asset that is critical to your mid- to long-term success, it is best to go for acquisition. This will allow you to secure the capability long term. When, however, this capability is important only in the short to mid term and may be obsolete quite soon or is not mission critical (in other words, good alternatives are available), then you should instead go for a partnership agreement. This will allow you to retain more flexibility. It will also tie up fewer assets.

MOVING TO ACTION: QUESTIONS TO ASK YOURSELF

- ✓ Taking a mid- to long-term view, how will the competitive landscape in your industry evolve? How will customer demands change? Are you well prepared? Which capabilities are you lacking?
- ✓ How can you build those missing capabilities? Organically in-house? Do partnerships make sense? Or are acquisitions the better way to go?
- ✓ Where should you and your team look for acquisition targets (also outside your industry)? How can you screen potential candidates?
- ✓ How can you start building your M&A muscle?

39. Summary: Key Insights and Action Plan

Use these two pages to capture the thoughts, epiphanies, revenue and profit ideas that came to your head when reading the last couple of chapters. Take 20 minutes to jot down the ideas. You will find that this time is very well invested. We will refer to this summary at the end of the book.

Book Section: "Drive Innovation and Growth"

My Action Plan

- ✓ Epiphanies/aha moments from this section: ……………..
  ………………………………………………………………...…..
  …………………………………………………………………..…
  …………………………………………………………………..…
  …………………………………………………………………..…
  …………………………………………………………………..…
  …………………………………………………………………..…
  …………………………………………………………………..…
  …………………………………………………………………..…
  …………………………………………………………………..…

- ✓ What I will immediately start implementing with my team as of next Monday morning: ……………………………….
  ………………………………………………………………..……

....
....
....
....
....
....
....
....
....
....

- ✓ Game-changing ideas that require thought and careful preparation. Assign a Board member to prepare a proposal on how to best implement/capture max benefits: ....

....
....
....
....
....
....
....
....
....
....
....

REACH PEAK PERFORMANCE

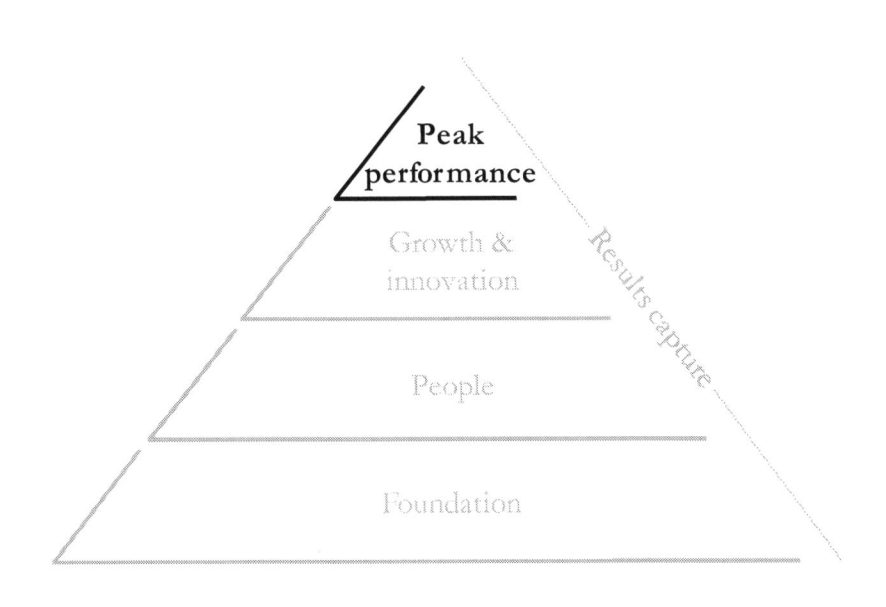

```
        /Peak
       /performance
      /─────────────
     /  Growth &       Results capture
    /   innovation
   /─────────────────
  /      People
 /───────────────────
/      Foundation
─────────────────────
```

40. THE 12-WEEK YEAR

> *"We mistakenly believe that there is a lot of time left in the year, and we act accordingly. We lack a sense of urgency, not realizing that every week is important, every day is important, every moment is important. Ultimately, effective execution happens daily and weekly!"*
> — Brian P. Moran, Michael Lennington

Let's run a quick test. Step outside your office and ask 10 colleagues when they did their Christmas shopping last year: (1) A few days before Christmas, (2) A few weeks before Christmas, (3) Already a couple of months before Christmas. I bet that the vast majority of your colleagues will give the first response. Why is that? And how is this relevant to your business?

It's relevant because the same thing also happens day in and day out at work. Let's assume it is Monday. You give one of your coworkers the task to prepare a report by Friday, end of day. You will experience that he will likely do the bulk of the work on Friday. Or your spouse asks you to get something for your son's birthday party from a local shop. The party is on Saturday afternoon. You will likely get the task done Saturday morning.

> ## 10x Results "Million $ Idea"
>
> If you give your team three months to complete an important project, it will take three months. If you give them one month, it will take one month. **We, humans, take as much time for a task as we are given; if you give double the time, people will take double the time.**
>
> Interestingly enough, often the **quality of the output will be better if you give people less time because they are more focused on the task.**
>
> So, the message is: **Set ambitious deadlines. They should be doable if focused effort is applied.** And they should not be arbitrary (asking for a report by Friday that you only need three weeks from now undermines morale and, generally, is not proper management).

So, what is the main point? Set ambitious deadlines on the important deliverables. Get people to focus their time and energy on these tasks. Deprioritize everything that is not mission critical. People will fill up their days with low-priority work—and they will get something done—but not something that is mission critical. Make sure that they spend their time doing mission-critical work.

How does this relate to the 12-week year? We all have a mental picture of what a person or a company can accomplish in a year. This notion is also factored into the New Year's resolutions or company plans that we prepare. Then, very soon, those important priorities get lost in the craze of the day to day. Don't let this happen to your business. Here is how you do it:

CHECKLIST: YOUR 12-WEEK YEAR

- ✓ **Mission-critical goals for the year:** What are the three to five mission-critical goals that, if you were to achieve them by the end of the year, would make this year into a great year? Write them down. This could be a new product release, or a market entry into China, or a 20 percentage point improvement in customer NPS.

- ✓ **What would it take:** Now, ask yourself the question: "What would it take to achieve these goals by the end of the quarter?" Bear with me for a second and do not disregard this question right away. Ask yourself: "If these were our only goals for quarter end, how would we tackle them? Who do we need to put on the task? How would we structure it? How would we track progress and course-correct?" Next, ask yourself which lower-value tasks and goals could be stopped or deprioritized to give these goals more time and resources? These are powerful questions, and you will see that what seemed impossible only a few moments back now becomes more realistic.

- ✓ **Action plan:** Clearly, an important goal on a tight timeline needs to be managed accordingly. Prepare a three to four-page project charter: What are the key sub-deliverables along the way (and what are the deadlines)? Which people do we put on the task? Which other resources do we need to invest? How do we steer the project?

If you do not want to go all-in yet, I dare you to test this approach at least with a division, product line, or with one of your countries. You will see that it works wonders. You will get the all-important stuff done much faster. And you will realize that many of the lower-priority tasks at the end do not need to be done after all.

Moving to Action: Questions to Ask Yourself

- ✓ In which area of your business do you want to test the 12-week-year approach?
- ✓ How do you get your key people's buy-in to the approach? Put them in the driver's seat?
- ✓ How do you track progress and fine-tune the approach?

41. Strategy-on-a-Page

> *"Too often, a company's strategy sits on a shelf, gathering dust. A strategy that doesn't influence critical decisions on a day-to-day basis, however, is not a strategy—it is a book report."*
>
> — Donald Sull

Do you remember your company's strategy? Can you recite it? Can your employees? If you are like many other CEOs and senior managers, the answer to at least one of those questions is likely "not sure." For many companies, a strategy is a set of documents that get prepared in the first six months of a new CEO joining. And then they get put away. They seldom guide day-to-day decisions and actions. That's a pity.

Let's start at the highest level: A company's strategy should be simple; it should fit on a poster that you can put in people's offices or as background images on their laptop screens. It should be emotional. It should have teeth. It should get people out of bed early and keep them working focused throughout the day.

10x Results "Million $ Idea"

Here is a SAMPLE of a "STRATEGY-ON-A-PAGE:"

"OUR COMPANY IS **ON THIS PLANET TO HELP ERADICATE CANCER** BY 2050. WE WORK CLOSELY WITH HEALTHCARE PROFESSIONALS TO SIGNIFICANTLY **IMPROVE THE LIVES OF PATIENTS AND THEIR FAMILIES**. WE HAVE THE **BEST SCIENTISTS** ON OUR

> *TEAM TO RESEARCH THE ROOT CAUSES AND **DEVELOP HIGHLY EFFECTIVE TREATMENTS AT AFFORDABLE COSTS**. WE DO SO BY **PARTNERING WITH EACH OTHER AND ALSO OUTSIDE EXPERTS**. WE SUCCEED BECAUSE OF OUR **SMART PEOPLE, OUR COLLABORATIVE APPROACH, AND OUR OUT-OF-THE-BOX THINKING**. WE NEVER TAKE NO FOR AN ANSWER, BUT ALWAYS DIG ONE LEVEL DEEPER."*
>
> In the few lines above, you can see **(1) the company's purpose/mission statement, (2) where they chose to play, and (3) how they believe they will win**. It is **emotional** and **concise**. It can be **put on posters** around the office. People will be able to **internalize it** within a few days. This alone will take you a long way toward **inspiring your people and guiding good decision making** on the day-to-day job.

Let's break down the elements of a good "strategy-on-a-page" statement for you:

Checklist: The Key Elements of a Great "Strategy-on-a-Page"

- ✓ **Your purpose/mission:** Getting out of bed and giving it your best day after day is hard—for you and especially for your employees. Unless your team has a strong enough reason to go the extra mile, they will likely slow down and slack off after a while. Your purpose and mission need to have strong, emotional pull power. Not all companies may be able to have a mission statement like "eradicate cancer by 2050," but statements like "help good families find and get their dream homes where they can share great memories together" are

good and have pull power.
- ✓ **Where to play:** It is crucial that you are clear on where to play and, even more important, where NOT to play. Which customers will you serve? And which will you not serve? What products and services will you offer? And what products and services will you not offer? Answering these questions and sticking to them will give you and your team strong guidance in the day-to-day activities.
- ✓ **How to win:** Will you have the best quality product? Will you have the greatest design? Will you have the best and most responsive customer service? Will you provide the best customer experience? Will you provide the lowest prices? Will you get your products or services to the customer fastest? Being clear on your positioning in the market and then making sure that you are CLEARLY perceived as number one on the dimensions you chose to excel in will help you to win in this market.

With these dimensions in mind, it is now a good time to reassess your own strategy statement. Obviously, there are different models to make money and be successful. So, there is no one size fits all here. But to help you get started, I have listed a few questions that will help you to pressure-test your current strategy. Is it strong? Is it inspirational? Does it allow you to profitably grow your business?

MOVING TO ACTION: QUESTIONS TO ASK YOURSELF

- ✓ Is your mission statement/company purpose strong? Does it get your people out of bed and excited to go to work? Does it touch them on an emotional level? Is it easy to understand?
- ✓ Did you clearly define where to play and where not to play (which customers/products/services)? Are you 100 percent sure that you can be THE preeminent number one player in this market (customers think of you first)? If there is no

chance of you getting into this position anytime within the next two to three years, then you may have to adjust where you play. Do you need to define your target market more narrowly? Can you be the preeminent number one then?

- ✓ Are you clear on how you will win versus the competition (i.e., best product, best service, best price, etc.)? Are these dimensions relevant and decisive for customers? Can you get there? Can you stay there? What is your profit generation model? Is it sustainable?

42. Management Board and Decision Effectiveness

"The best way to predict the future is to create it."
— Peter Drucker

Think back to your last two or three Board meetings. How much time did you spend on functional updates? Too much? And how much time did you spend on an in-depth, two-hour discussion of one of your key strategic priorities (leading to measurable progress and clear decisions)? Too little?

I'm guessing that your answer is that most of the time was spent rushing through functional updates, with little discussion on the truly important strategic priorities. And if there was a discussion, it was mainly between two people—the CEO and the functional owner. Rarely was there a debate where more than half of the Board members were actively involved. Many decisions were either postponed or, if reached, reopened in the next meeting.

This is a pity and a waste of valuable resources. You have the most valuable (and highest-paid) people in the room, you should use this time to make significant advances on the most critical priorities of the company. Here are a few strategies to increase the effectiveness of your Board meetings:

Checklist: Making Your Board Meetings Much More Effective

- ✓ **Spend at least half of the meeting time discussing your three to five "game-changing" strategic initiatives:** You have the brightest minds of the company in the room. Use them to discuss these topics in depth to drive your profitable growth over the next one to three years. This could be, for example, your project to set up a new "urban product line" that is planned to contribute 25 percent to your bottom line three years from now. Or it could be the vital product quality turnaround initiative that will help you drive down the massive product returns and stop customer losses. Or it could be the market entry Asia initiative that is projected to contribute another 25 percent to your bottom line three years from now. Spend at least two to three hours discussing each of these topics. Only when you allocate sufficient time and get people to participate can you expect a meaningful discussion. You and your team will be surprised at how much progress you can make when you are focused. And make sure that you actually make decisions and take note of the agreed actions at the end of the discussion.
- ✓ **Distribute pre-read materials two to three business days before meeting:** Include all functional updates in the pre-read materials.
- ✓ **Functional flashlight:** Reduce the functional updates to "functional flashlights." Spend a max of 20 minutes each. Spend the first 10 minutes on the most important action items for the group. You need no more than one slide for this. Spend the remaining 10 minutes on discussing any questions that the group may have on the functional pre-read materials.
- ✓ **Short and crisp minutes and follow-up:** Distribute meeting minutes at the latest one day after the meeting. Document ac-

tions and decisions clearly. Follow up at the next Board meeting on all actions. Put people on the spot, if needed. This will happen only once.

- ✓ **Physical presence only once a quarter:** For many global (and even regional) Board meetings, you will have situations where more than half of the Board members need to travel two days to get to a one-day Board meeting. This is a waste of their time and the company's resources. Have everybody in for an in-person meeting once a quarter followed by a team dinner and team bonding activity. Otherwise, leverage video conferencing. Keep the video calls to a max of four hours. Manage one-on-one topics in one-on-one calls; take them out of your Board meetings with the entire team.

- ✓ **Two sets of Board meetings:** A good practice is to have two sets of Board meetings: One set with your functional direct reports where you can prepare the functional priority topics. These are not decision meetings. They are to prepare the initiatives for discussion and decision. The second set is the all-hands Board meeting with the functional direct reports and also the regional/country/business unit heads. This is the meeting where all major initiatives are discussed and decided upon. You could have these two sets of meetings alternating (one month the functional Board meeting happens, and the other month the full Board meeting happens).

- ✓ **Active participation:** Every person who attends should have a visible role in the meeting. Rule of thumb: at least 10 percent of the meeting time should be active talking time for any person in the meeting. Otherwise, you should ask yourself whether this person needs to attend the meeting.

- ✓ **Limit CEO talking time:** Many CEOs tend to dominate the Board meetings, some with more than 50 percent of speaking time. Try to get it down to around 20 percent. Empower your people; get them out of their comfort zone.

One more thing: Try to reduce the number of your functional heads to five or six max. Two of them are typically your CFO and your head of sales and marketing. For the other functions (and this also includes IT, HR, products, strategy, transformation, etc.), try to combine them in a way that makes sense among three to four people. Having too many functional heads increases the decision-making complexity exponentially and creates waste (too many people have to attend too many calls and meetings).

10x Results "Million $ Idea"

One of the most **destructive habits in many companies is the inability to stick to decisions.** Decisions that have been made and even minuted get reopened for some reasons: Key stakeholder not present, new facts on the table, after-the-fact disagreement with the decision. Don't let this happen at your company.

(1) Include in the agenda for the meeting a **list of the decisions** that are planned to be made.

(2) Advise that the **decision will be made** in the meeting. If a stakeholder is not present, then she should submit her input and vote beforehand, for consideration during the discussion.

(3) Allow for **enough time to discuss all facets** of the topic and then **decide on it.**

(4) As a final step, after the decision is made, look at everybody in the room and make an **explicit statement**

> **THAT YOU EXPECT THE DECISION TO BE FINAL AND TO BE EXECUTED UPON.**

MOVING TO ACTION: QUESTIONS TO ASK YOURSELF

- ✓ How can you restructure your Board meetings so that the majority of time is spent on in-depth discussions of the major strategic initiatives (with clear and agreed-upon decisions at the end)?
- ✓ How can you ensure effective decision-making and decision-adherence culture?
- ✓ If you had to cut down your Board meeting time in half, where would you start (reduced frequency, reduced time per meeting, reduced set of participants, reduce functional updates, more video calls instead of physical meetings)?
- ✓ For each Board meeting, do you know what the five to seven key decisions are that you need to make in this meeting? How can you structure the meeting in a way that those decisions get made and are later adhered to?

43. The Role of Active Investors and Outside Directors

"The price of greatness is responsibility."
— Winston S. Churchill

Over the last two decades and notably since the fall of Enron and the global financial crisis in 2008 and 2009, the responsibilities of the Board of Directors have significantly increased. And so has the scrutiny. I am not here to write about all the duties of the Board and its subcommittees. I am here to write about how I believe an effective Board, and especially its outside, independent directors and active investors, can contribute the greatest to the success of the company.

10x Results "Million $ Idea"

To achieve and sustain great company success, the **Board of Directors has three main duties:**

(1) Put the **right people into leadership** roles.

(2) Ensure an **ambitious company strategy** that mobilizes the organization, creates massive value for customers, and sustains profitable growth for shareholders.

(3) Ensure **discipline and hold executives accountable** for realizing that ambition.

In the table below, I have summarized the key elements for each of these three main duties.

CHECKLIST: THREE MAIN DUTIES OF ACTIVE INVESTORS AND OUTSIDE DIRECTORS TO ENSURE COMPANY SUCCESS

- ✓ **Put the right people into leadership roles:** What should you be looking for in a senior executive? What does it take to successfully lead a company or division? As I wrote in earlier chapters, I believe that character is the most important trait in a senior executive—integrity, resilience, humility, the ability to listen and inspire action. Next, come energy and vitality. This is a dimension that is often overlooked, but tired, exhausted, burned-out executives do your company no good. Last on the list comes the technical expertise for the job—industry and functional know-how. Don't get me wrong, these are very important, but if the first two traits are not in place, then industry and functional knowledge will have little effect.
- ✓ **Ensure an ambitious company strategy:** "Why not? Why not faster? Why not more?" These are some of the questions that you should be asking. Aiming for the average is easy. To aim for what the market expects or just a bit more is easy. Your job is to get the executive team to develop, believe in, and commit to a strategy that delivers exceptional value to customers and in turn also to shareholders. It also mobilizes the troops to do their greatest. Raising expectations and holding the executive team to extremely high standards is, therefore, one of your most important jobs.
- ✓ **Ensure discipline and hold executives accountable:** An ambitious strategy is excellent, but the battle is won in the day

to day. What ambitious milestones did the executive team commit to achieving by the end of the quarter? Did they do it? Why not? What needs to be done to course-correct? Is there a fundamental problem with the ability of the executive team to execute? If yes, how can this be fixed quickly?

Active investors and outside directors are in this sense like good sports coaches. They set the bar very high. They drive their athletes to excel. They ensure that they have the right support system. They ensure that progress gets tracked diligently. And they celebrate with the athletes when success is achieved.

MOVING TO ACTION: QUESTIONS TO ASK YOURSELF

- ✓ Do you have the right people on the bus? Are the wrong people off the bus? If not, what is your strategy to correct this?
- ✓ Is your game plan for the next three years extraordinarily ambitious, but yet—with focused execution—achievable? If not, what is your plan to either up the ambition level or operationalize the game plan to ensure achievability?
- ✓ How do you ensure focused execution? Do people know exactly what is expected of them? Do they exactly know how success will be measured?

44. Build Your Organizational Muscle

> *"You can't hire someone else to do your push-ups for you."*
>
> — Jim Rohn

One of your key responsibilities as a leader is to allow (even to demand) your people to grow. In sports, growth happens when you put stress on your muscles—run a bit faster, swim a bit longer, jump a bit higher. This is how muscles grow. And this is also how your organizational muscle grows.

10x Results "Million $ Idea"

Many companies see their **change initiatives fail because the organization is not used to change.** When they have never done it, it's tough for people to change their habits.

To avoid this, build your organizational "change muscle" with small change initiatives that your organization can digest. Do this repeatedly, and then, **gradually, your "change muscle" will grow.**

CHECKLIST: HOW TO BUILD ORGANIZATIONAL MUSCLE

- ✓ **Small change initiatives:** Many companies see their change efforts fail, because the organization is just not used to change. When you have never had to experience significant change (at least not for the last two to four years), it becomes very hard for people to change. To counter this and build "change muscle," implement smaller changes on a regular basis: a new electronic document management system or a new lead generation process. Over time, these smaller change initiatives will allow your people to get used to change so that when the more significant changes happen, the organization is ready.
- ✓ **Put your people in the driver's seat:** Some companies rely heavily on external consultants to manage their large programs (cost cutting, growth, IT implementation, etc.). While the outside expertise and the additional set of hands are generally good, it also sometimes inhibits your own people from growing. Make sure that all initiatives are led by your people and that external support is used sparingly and where it helps most (a good ratio is that max 25 percent of the program team is composed of external consultants). The benefit of this approach is that you increase buy-in from your people since they have been driving the effort.
- ✓ **Growth assignments:** Ensure that you put everybody on growth assignments. This is not just for your top 10 percent who typically get those assignments, but for the entire organization. You want everybody to stretch a little (according to their abilities). This way you build muscle and flexibility at all organizational levels.

MOVING TO ACTION: QUESTIONS TO ASK YOURSELF

- ✓ Do you have enough "change muscle?" Does your organization usually deal well with change efforts? If not, what are some small-scale change programs that you can use to build organizational "change muscle?"
- ✓ Are you overly reliant on external consultants? As a test, if you would take them out from one day to the next, would important programs or parts of your business go south? If so, how can you get your own employees to gradually take more responsibility?
- ✓ Are all of your people stretching and learning new things? This is not about doing more of the same thing, but instead, learning new skills. If you are not sure, then this is a clear indicator that more needs to be done. Keep it small, keep it informal, keep it fun. Don't make this into a bureaucratic monster.

45. Make Use of New Technology/Digitalization

> *"One machine can do the work of fifty ordinary men. No machine can do the work of one extraordinary man."*
> — Elbert Hubbard

Blockchain, big data/advanced analytics, artificial intelligence, machine learning—it becomes increasingly difficult for executives to stay on top of technological advances. It seems like every new technological buzz will radically change the profit pools in many industries. So, what should top executives do?

10x Results "Million $ Idea"

It almost never pays off to be a first mover on new technologies (even if you are a tech company), unless this is your core business. Many technologies will radically change until they are commercially viable at a larger scale in your business. So, avoid jumping on every technological bandwagon.

Instead, make sure that you leverage existing, mature technologies to the greatest degree. I am talking about handy stuff like video conferencing, electronic data management, and collaboration platforms. These may sound extremely "unsexy," and this is because they are. They will not get you *Wall Street Journal*

> HEADLINES, BUT THEY **WILL SIGNIFICANTLY CONTRIBUTE TO YOUR BOTTOM LINE** (FAR MORE THAN MANY OF THE NEW, HOT TECHNOLOGIES COULD AT THE MOMENT).

CHECKLIST: TECHNOLOGIES THAT MOST COMPANIES SHOULD LEVERAGE

- ✓ **Start with the basics:** A laptop that works and starts quickly. Good network connection. Excellent collaboration and work software (i.e., Office, Skype for Business, Slack). No access to private social media (i.e., Facebook, Instagram, Twitter) while at work. Network printing and scanning. It's the easy, mundane stuff that is most often neglected but brings the most significant benefits to the bottom line. Fix this stuff and you will see immediate benefits.

- ✓ **Reduce travel time and cost:** When a senior executive travels cross-continental to a business meeting, the total costs to the company can easily run to $10,000 or more (travel, hotel, downtime). Now, the business case is simple: Reduce internal (non-customer) meetings by more than 50 percent by installing good video-conferencing equipment in your major sites. There are immersive telepresence solutions now available that will feel like you are indeed in one room. Use Skype for Business or similar apps on laptops. Ensure sufficient bandwidth, and you are good to go. To ensure compliance, require signoff from senior executives on travel for internal meetings.

- ✓ **Use IP telephony:** Migrate your expense PBX telephony solution (equipment, system, call minutes) to IP telephony. Get rid of most desk phones—route calls either to cell phones or laptop computers. Use visual voicemail. Get people decent

headsets. Test data calls on and off premises.
- ✓ **Reduce email and duplicated data storage:** Many managers and executives get more than 200 emails a day. It is ineffective to have half of your top management team spend two hours or more a day on email when in many cases only 10 percent of the emails are critical and require their urgent attention. Implement an electronic document management system. Use collaboration platforms (like Microsoft Teams, SharePoint). They now also come with instant messaging features and allow you to keep all documents and team conversations in one place. The benefits include: (1) Always the most up-to-date documents, (2) Full access and searchability to team discussions, (3) Central task management, (4) Significantly less email, (5) Significantly less data traffic and data storage, and the list goes on. This technology is ready—use it.
- ✓ **Email best practices:** For the email that remains, allow people to reduce the time they spend on it by more than half by teaching them how to use auto rules, auto email formatting, sorting by conversations, email search features, and effective, crisp email writing techniques.

Coming back to the topic of "super-hot" new technologies: While you will not have to implement them right away, you should still make sure that you keep on top of those new technologies. You (or your key people) should know what technological advances are around the corner and how you could profit from them a few years from now. Keep your eye on blockchain, big data, AI, machine learning, and all the other new technological advances. And when the time is right, move. Here are a few simple rules to help guide your thinking:

> ## 10x Results "Million $ Idea"
>
> When you look at it from the perspective of the **technology adoption lifecycle**, the advice for 95 percent of businesses is:
>
> (1) Never be a **first mover** (unless this is your core business).
>
> (2) Be an **early adopter** of those technologies that (a) you genuinely understand and that (b) provide a sustainable competitive advantage to your business.
>
> (3) Be among the **early majority for most relevant technologies** (at a time when they are maturing, cost-effective, and stable); still a few months earlier than your competitors.
>
> (4) Never be a **laggard or among the late majority** for relevant technologies.

Moving to Action: Questions to Ask Yourself

- ✓ Have you implemented all the beneficial mature technologies that are mentioned above? If not, how can you speed up the implementation to start reaping the benefits?
- ✓ Which new technologies could be a key competitive differentiator for you? How do you track them? Should you "micro test" them in your organization (to learn and pilot/pressure-test the business case)?

46. Summary: Key Insights and Action Plan

Use these two pages to capture the thoughts, epiphanies, revenue and profit ideas that came to your head when reading the last couple of chapters. Take 20 minutes to jot down the ideas. You will find that this time is very well invested. We will refer to this summary at the end of the book.

Book Section: "Reach Peak Performance"
My Action Plan

- ✓ Epiphanies/aha moments from this section: ....
  ....
  ....
  ....
  ....
  ....
  ....
  ....
  ....
  ....

- ✓ What I will immediately start implementing with my team as of next Monday morning: ....
  ....

....
....
....
....
....
....
....
....
....
....

✓ **Game-changing ideas that require thought and careful preparation. Assign a Board member to prepare a proposal on how to best implement/capture max benefits:** ....
....
....
....
....
....
....
....
....
....
....
....

Results Capture / How to Implement

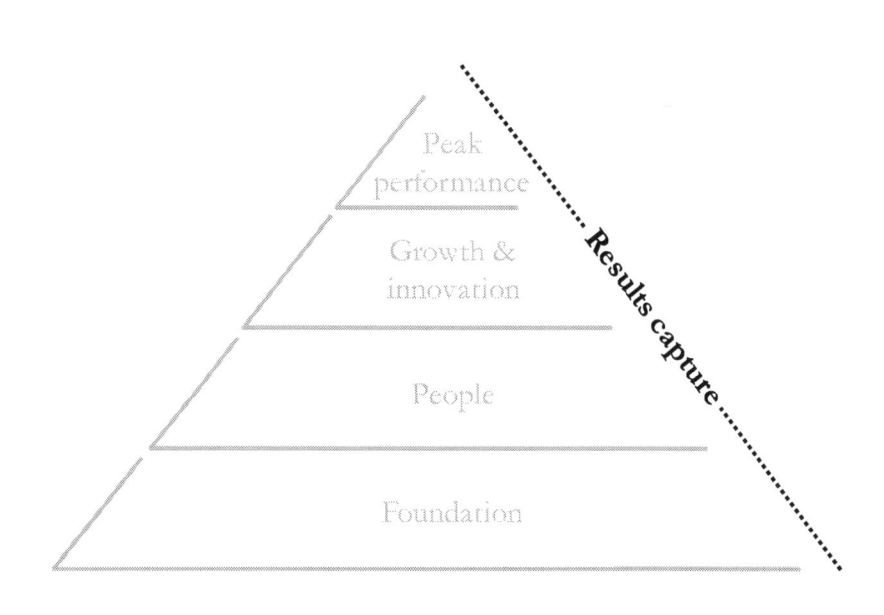

47. How to Prioritize/Where to Start

> *"The key is not to prioritize what's on your schedule, but to schedule your priorities."*
> — Stephen Covey

The 10x Results approach needs to be seen as an integrated whole where all elements tie into and complement each other. Therefore, to achieve truly outstanding results, it is essential to implement the individual initiatives in a synchronized way. For example, applying the principles from "focus, focus, focus" and "reduce complexity and cut waste" will allow you to free up your people's time and mental energy, which, in turn, can then be used to drive the innovation and growth initiatives.

Having said this, the beauty of the 10x Results approach is that it is at the same time very flexible. All initiatives can be implemented individually. While this will not give you the cumulative benefits from the integrated approach, it will yield significant benefits. Especially in situations where you believe that your business is generally doing great but significantly falling behind in two or three areas, it is okay to start with these high-priority areas. If, for example, you believe that your pain point areas are "insane customer focus," "deep work," and "making meetings and conference calls more effective," then start there.

There is a best practice sequence of implementing the 10x Results initiatives. First, work on getting the "foundation" right. This will allow you to become more focused and free up your employees' time. Second, work on the "people" topics—aiming to multiply the effectiveness and efficiency of all your employees. Third, use this focus to ignite the "innovation and growth" engine. Last, but not least, top it off with the capstone initiatives "reach peak performance."

The ideal implementation sequence would look like the picture below. The timeline may vary depending on company size. For mid-size companies, two to three years is realistic. For some Fortune 500 companies, it may take up to five years. For smaller startups, the whole approach can be implemented within a year.

10X RESULTS APPROACH: SEQUENCING THE INITIATIVES FOR MAXIMUM IMPACT

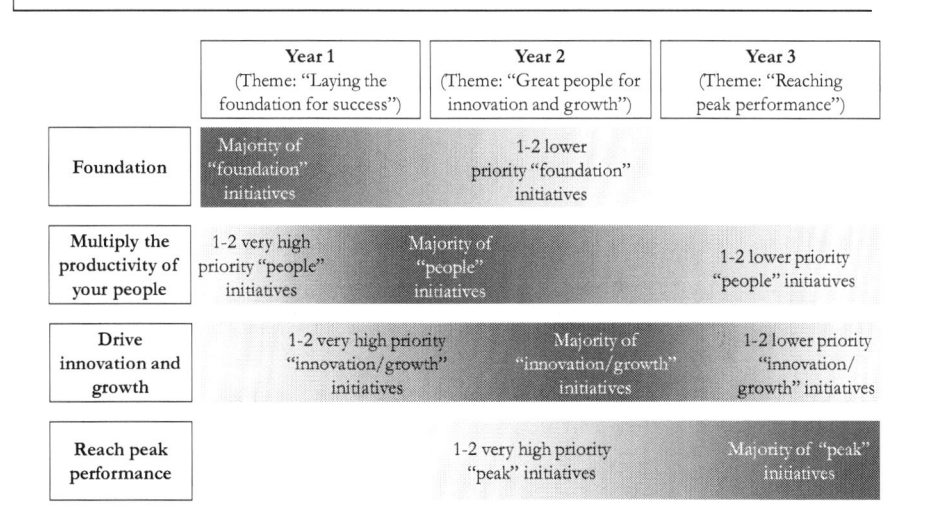

	Year 1 (Theme: "Laying the foundation for success")	Year 2 (Theme: "Great people for innovation and growth")	Year 3 (Theme: "Reaching peak performance")
Foundation	Majority of "foundation" initiatives	1-2 lower priority "foundation" initiatives	
Multiply the productivity of your people	1-2 very high priority "people" initiatives	Majority of "people" initiatives	1-2 lower priority "people" initiatives
Drive innovation and growth	1-2 very high priority "innovation/growth" initiatives	Majority of "innovation/growth" initiatives	1-2 lower priority "innovation/growth" initiatives
Reach peak performance		1-2 very high priority "peak" initiatives	Majority of "peak" initiatives

This approach gives you a significant level of flexibility. For example, if you believe that the two initiatives "Give your team a why" and "Hire and keep only A players" from the "people" layer are extremely important and would give your company a boost, then prioritize them together with the "foundation" initiatives.

> ## 10X RESULTS "MILLION $ IDEA"
>
> THE MOST IMPORTANT THING IS TO **NOT OVERPLAN IT, BUT TO START**. PICK THE **HIGHEST-GAIN INITIATIVES FROM THE "FOUNDATION" LAYER** AND TOP THEM OFF WITH THE **ONE OR TWO HIGHEST IMPACT INITIATIVES FROM THE "PEOPLE" LAYER**. ENSURE THAT AT LEAST TWO INITIATIVES ALLOW YOU TO **REALIZE QUICK WINS** (VISIBLE BENEFITS WITHIN THE NEXT THREE MONTHS). THAT'S IT. YOU'RE GOOD TO GO.
>
> **REVIEW AFTER THREE MONTHS** WHERE YOU'RE AT, AND SLIGHTLY ADJUST IF NEEDED. THIS WAY YOU WILL ACHIEVE MUCH MORE MUCH FASTER, THAN IF YOU HAD OVERPLANNED IT.

While you do this, three aspects require careful consideration.

CHECKLIST: ASPECTS TO CONSIDER WHEN PRIORITIZING THE INITIATIVES

- ✓ **Readiness for change:** In some organizations, change efforts can be implemented faster—in others, it takes more time. You need to find your sweet spot. Going too fast will overburden the organization. Going too slow will stall the change. Look at the magnitude of changes that your company has undergone over the past three to five years. This will give you a good indication. Also, younger companies and founder-led companies are typically able to implement changes faster.
- ✓ **Quick wins AND maximum total benefits:** You need the right mix between quick-win initiatives that quickly show very positive results in the eyes of your employees and more structural fixing initiatives that require the organization to endure

more, but also come with higher benefits. Ensure that you keep a good balance.
- ✓ **Economic climate:** The general sequence of the 10x Results initiatives is independent of whether you are in a boom or recession. For example, in a recession it makes sense to start with the "foundation" and "people" initiatives because this will allow you to take out costs quickly. The same applies to a boom period. Jumping two steps and starting with "innovation and growth" without a solid "foundation" and "people" structure sets you up for failure when the next recession hits. The only exception is initiatives that require significant capital investment, which are more on the "innovation and growth" side. Here you will want to be careful during a recession.

It is crucial that you get in successes early—to keep your people motivated and moving. Below is a list of the initiatives that will allow you to realize positive results quickly; employees will see measurable improvements in their day-to-day work.

CHECKLIST: QUICK-WIN INITIATIVES

- ✓ **Focus, focus, focus:** By deciding relatively quickly on what not to do going forward, your employees will experience more clarity and less distraction from low-priority topics. They will be able to focus on the "biggies" and, thus, also become more engaged.
- ✓ **Getting better every day:** Creating a process and an environment to realize frequent, small improvements has a positive impact on employee morale. The ability to give input and see this input taken into account will also increase their sense of ownership.
- ✓ **Make your meetings and conference calls 10 times more effective:** Meetings and conference calls are some of the big-

gest annoyances in most companies. The principles by which to optimize them are relatively easy to implement and show results quickly. Your people will love it.

- ✓ **Publicly recognize and praise excellent performance:** All this initiative takes to implement is a mindset shift by your senior managers. Commenting positively on a job well done can make an employee's day (or even week). Lead by example, and you will see that soon all senior managers will follow.
- ✓ **Keep your people's energy levels high:** You do not need to implement the full enchilada. But encouraging "walk meetings," having "fruit and veggie baskets," offering good herbal tea, getting people wireless headsets so that they can walk while being on a conference call, encouraging employee groups for running, basketball, and all other kinds of sports does not take much money or time, but shows visible results to the employees. (And you will also likely see a significant decline in employee sick days.)

MOVING TO ACTION: QUESTIONS TO ASK YOURSELF

- ✓ Does the general sequencing of initiatives makes sense for us? Which of the individual initiatives should we prioritize? Which ones can be put on the back burner?
- ✓ Do we need to adjust the speed of implementation (go faster or slower)?
- ✓ Which one or two of the proposed quick-win initiatives would give us the highest benefits? Can we start with them right away?

48. Effectively Manage Change and Bring in Results

"Be the change that you wish to see in the world."
— Mahatma Gandhi

Why do people resist change? What makes it so hard for them? Thinking of the major change efforts in your company, try to answer these questions? When you think 10 to 20 years back, how did you experience the change efforts that other managers put in? What were your feelings? What did those managers handle well? And what did they handle poorly?

Answering these questions for yourself will give you an excellent understanding of the "inner dimensions of change." Change is hard. Especially when someone else imposes the change on you. But this is what happens in companies: Top management decides, and most employees feel left out and, therefore, become resistant to the change.

Fortunately, there are a few things that you can do to significantly increase the odds of your change effort going through successfully. This is not "smoke and mirrors," but addressing change at its emotional heart. Here they are:

Checklist: The Key Ingredients to Ensure Success in Every Change Effort

- ✓ **Ensure buy-in of senior executives and key multipliers throughout the organization:** Before you start any significant change effort, make sure that you have the full support from your senior executives and managers. Create buy-in by involving them early in the definition of the "why," "where to," and "how." You can do this by taking one day from the agenda in your next company management conference. Have them co-create the why/where to/how in a workshop setting. Once you have a solid draft, involve and enlist the support of other key multipliers in the organization. Do not proceed to any of the next steps before you have accomplished this step.
- ✓ **Explain the WHY:** Change is difficult and hard to experience on a personal and emotional level. Without a clear and compelling case on why to change, your change effort will stall. Some examples of reasons for the change: "We are burning millions every quarter; if we do not reverse this trend, we will be out of business within the next two years," "Our industry will change completely over the next 10 years; we need to get out of optical film reels ASAP and double down on digital production technology or cease to exist five years from now."
- ✓ **Show the WHERE TO in an emotional way:** The destination/target picture needs to be vivid. Apply the "tear of joy in the eyes" test. Example: "We will be the company to cure liver cancer; fifty years from now, people around the world will still remember our team."
- ✓ **Communicate the HOW and have a clear execution playbook:** Have a clear implementation plan with deliverables, milestones, resources, steering and issue resolution mechanisms, capability build-up plan, resistance anticipation,

and resolution playbook. This plan needs to be balanced against what the organization can deliver (i.e., what amount of change it can endure).

- ✓ **Clear message and communication:** Your message needs to be simple, memorable, consistent, and emotional, with vivid pictures and metaphors—and repeated over and over again. It needs to include the elements of why/where to/how. It also needs to explicitly answer "what is in it for me?" on a personal level for all employees. Similarly, it needs to spell out what behavioral change is expected from each and every employee. Regarding communication channels, do not just broadcast, but go down to the team level. Use: (1) Message from the CEO/the Board, (2) Town hall meetings with Q&A, (3) Central information hub, (4) Manager/team meetings.
- ✓ **Ensure early successes:** A transformation that is all uphill will get stuck at some point. Ensure that you can present success stories that measurably improve your employees' lives every couple of months. Three months is a good interval. So, when you schedule your transformation program, make sure that certain sub-initiatives show results after three, six, nine, 12 months, and so on.
- ✓ **Get feedback and address critiques:** Ensure open, direct, and timely feedback from your employees. I recommend using the Net Promoter Score also for this process. You can analyze this by department and seniority level. It should give you a good feel for where you're at. Allow verbatim feedback. Secondly, make sure that you openly address critique from employees. You can do this in a town hall setting, in the CEO call, in team meetings, or in the Q&As on the central transformation intranet hub.

While all of the points mentioned above are important, there is one element that stands out, and this is successfully answering the "why" question. If you give people a strong enough "why," they will be willing to endure a lot.

10x RESULTS "MILLION $ IDEA"

THE "WHY" IS THE GOLDEN KEY TO ANY SUCCESSFUL CHANGE EFFORT. THIS IS WHERE YOU START, AND THIS IS WHERE YOU FOCUS.

WHY DO WE HAVE TO CHANGE? **WHY** IS THIS INEVITABLE? **WHY** IS WHAT WE ARE DOING THE BEST OPTION? **WHY** IS THIS THE BEST **FOR ME**?

ANSWER THESE QUESTIONS FOR YOUR TEAM, AND YOU WILL ACHIEVE THE BUY-IN THAT YOU NEED TO SUCCESSFULLY LEAD THE CHANGE EFFORT.

COMMUNICATE. LISTEN. REACT WITH HONESTY TO WHAT YOUR PEOPLE TELL YOU. ADMIT THAT YOU DON'T HAVE ALL THE ANSWERS, BUT AT THE SAME TIME, DEMONSTRATE CONFIDENCE THAT THE APPROACH IS THE RIGHT ONE.

Make sure that you make your change management efforts an integral part of the overall transformation. In many companies, the top management underinvests in this area—saying that "they will get it eventually"—only to see that the overall transformation effort fails. Don't be one of them.

Moving to Action: Questions to Ask Yourself

- ✓ What is your experience with change efforts in your company over the past couple of years? How high was the resistance? What were the root causes? What was the best way to overcome the resistance?
- ✓ For the change efforts that you are currently planning, can you tick off all the points in the checklist above? With confidence? If you are not 100 percent sure, go back to the drawing table and see how you can get this fixed. It will significantly increase the ease, speed, and success of the transformation if you get all of these change management elements right.

49. Your Role as a Business Owner and CEO

"Be yourself; everyone else is already taken."
— Oscar Wilde

You do not need to buy 20 books on becoming a great CEO or business owner. You have all the answers in you already. You're not sure? Okay, then let's try: Take a minute to look back at some of your former bosses. Some may bring a smile to your face. What is it that you admired about them? What did they do or not do? How did they treat their people? What kind of person were they? What made them great? For the bosses you hated, what did they do wrong?

When you ask yourself these questions—and take some time to answer them—you should get a pretty vivid picture of what a great CEO/business owner should be like. Take 15 minutes to put the dos and don'ts on paper. There you are. Now, with all your actions throughout the day, try to be this person. Before going to bed, review how you stacked up against your ideal self. And work on the issues that require fixing the next day. Soon, you'll be surprised at the person you have become.

> ## 10x Results "Million $ Idea"
>
> **Understanding that you don't have to go it alone** is probably one of the most important realizations that you can have as a CEO or business owner.
>
> **You do not need to have all the answers.** You do not need to be smarter or better than everyone else. You do not need to work longer or harder. You do not need to sacrifice your family over work. You do not need to be tougher.
>
> It is actually quite the opposite: All of the above will not make you an effective CEO/business owner.
>
> **Asking questions. Listening. Enlisting support. Admitting when you're wrong. Relying on your team.** This is what will make you a great CEO/business owner.

When it comes to the job of CEO/business owner, it is not about technical skills anymore. You have proven that you know your stuff. You have proven that you can manage teams and work well with customers. You have proven that you have foresight and strategic vision. Now it is mainly a question of character that will allow you to become a great CEO.

Checklist: What Makes a Great CEO/Business Owner

- ✓ **Integrity and honesty:** People trust individuals who are open and honest. Who do not lie. Who have their interests at heart. Who do not sugarcoat. When your people see you this way, they will endure great pain and suffering because they trust you. This does not mean that you are weak. It means that you are a man or woman who people can look up to and aspire to become.
- ✓ **Ask and listen:** Avoid telling; telling makes YOU feel good, but everybody else feels terrible. Instead, ask open questions (What, why, how, etc.). "What do you think?" is one of the most powerful questions in the world. It creates buy-in and increases self-confidence.
- ✓ **Actions speak louder than words:** Be a role model for the behaviors that you want your people to emulate.
- ✓ **Delegate almost everything:** Do the things that only you can do and delegate everything else. Doing this will allow you to do those things that only you can do exceptionally well. And this will make all the difference. Don't try to be a better salesperson than your head of sales and marketing. Don't try to be a better CFO than your CFO. Don't try to be a better strategist than your head of strategy and corporate development. Get the best people into these roles and then let them do their job (do not micromanage and overpower the team discussions). You can then focus on doing your job exceptionally well.
- ✓ **Resilience:** Remain resilient and positive when the market turns south, when key people leave, and when you hear opposition. Resilience does not mean being stubborn, myopic, or overconfident. It means that you are able to endure pain without letting it out unfiltered on your people.

In the context of preparing and running a transformation program for your company, your role is much more about enlisting support/creating buy-in, explaining the "why" and creating a strong enough case for change (a "burning platform"). This should be your priority one, two, and three.

> **MOVING TO ACTION: QUESTIONS TO ASK YOURSELF**
> - ✓ What is the legacy that you want to leave for your company?
> - ✓ How can you inspire your people to join you to realize this legacy vision? This is now more a question of "who you need to become" and less a question of "what you need to say or do."
> - ✓ What is your step-by-step, day-by-day action plan to become the great CEO/business owner that you aspire to be? Who can support you on this journey (from within and outside your company)? How can you enlist their support?

50. Bringing It All Together—The 10x Results Action Plan

> *"A good plan violently executed now is better than a perfect plan executed next week."*
> — George S. Patton

Now is the moment of truth. The moment when we take all the lessons and insights from this book and put them into an action plan. Your action plan. The moment when you commit to action. I am thrilled and excited to take this step together with you.

The first step in creating a personal 10x Results action plan for your business is to again review your most valuable personal findings from each section in this book. Take 20 to 30 minutes to go back to the summary chapters at the end of each book section. Review your notes. What were your most valuable epiphanies/aha moments? What will you start implementing right away? What game-changing ideas require more thought and careful planning? Consolidate all ideas from the subsections of the book and put them onto the following two pages. Do not skip this step; it will make your action plan much more powerful.

Your Personal Synthesis of the Most Valuable Insights from the Book

✓ Most valuable epiphanies/aha moments from the book:..

....

....

....
....
....
....
....
....
....
....
....
....
....
....
....
....

- ✓ What I will immediately start implementing with my team as of "next Monday morning:" ....
....
....
....
....
....
....
....
....
....

....
....
....
....
....
....

✓ **Game-changing ideas that require thought and careful preparation. Will assign a Board member to prepare a proposal on how to best implement/capture max benefits:**
....
....
....
....
....
....
....
....
....
....
....
....
....
....

The next step is to prioritize each of the initiatives that we covered in this book. As mentioned in the chapter on "how to prioritize/where to start," I suggest that you mark one or two of the initiatives of each layer of the pyramid as "very high priority." Also, mark one or two of the initiatives of each layer as "low priority." Do these two steps first, then you will see which initiatives remain for the middle "priority" column. Now, take about 20 to 30 minutes to do this exercise for each of the four layers of the pyramid.

10X RESULTS APPROACH: PRIORITIZATION OF INITIATIVES

Layer 1: Foundation	Very high priority	Priority	Low priority
Focus, focus, focus			
Reduce complexity and cut waste			
Insane customer focus			
Getting better every day			
Measure success			
Bias for action			
Commit to a goal and stick to it			

Layer 2: People	Very high priority	Priority	Low priority
Give your team a "why" that is worth fighting for			
Set the bar high			
Hire and keep only A players			
Put your people into growth roles			
Delegate authority and hold people 100 percent accountable			
Make each day count			
Deep work			

10x Results: Multiply the Value of Your Business

Make your meetings and conference calls 10x more effective			
Money is not everything—publicly recognize and praise excellent performance			
Manage by deliverables, not tasks			
Keep your people's energy levels high			

Layer 3: Innovation and Growth	Very high priority	Priority	Low priority
A powerful framework for business growth			
Customer referrals and testimonials			
Punch above your weight: JVs/partnerships			
Become world class in winning new business			
Implement a world-class pricing model			
Take calculated risks			
Double down on innovation			
Put your growth on steroids: Use small-scale acquisitions to close capability gaps			

Layer 4: Peak Performance	Very high priority	Priority	Low priority
The 12-week year			
Strategy-on-a-page			
Management Board and decision effectiveness			
Role of active investors and outside directors			
Build your organizational muscle			
Make use of new technologies/Digitalization			

Next, please put the names of the very high-priority initiatives and the low-priority initiatives into the following action plan template.

Your 10x Results Action Plan

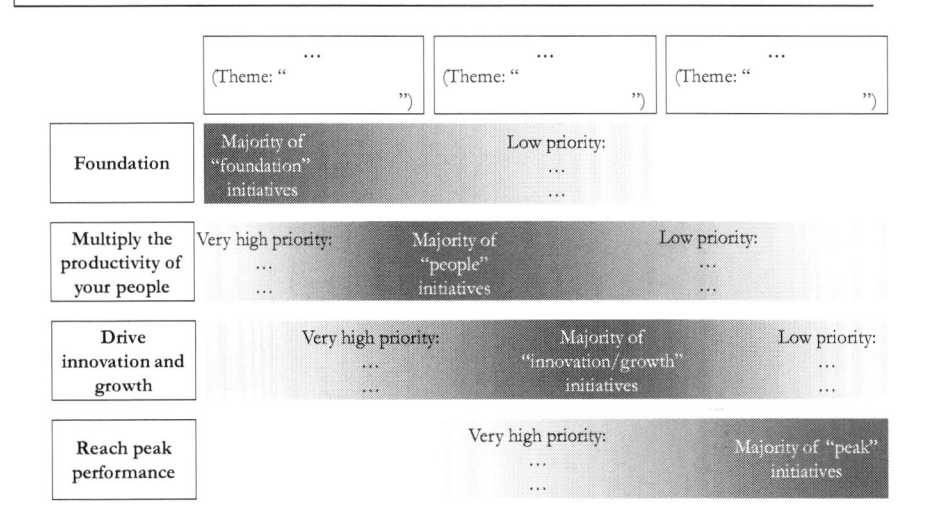

	(Theme: " ")	(Theme: " ")	(Theme: " ")
Foundation	Majority of "foundation" initiatives	Low priority: ...	
Multiply the productivity of your people	Very high priority:	Majority of "people" initiatives	Low priority: ... ...
Drive innovation and growth	Very high priority:	Majority of "innovation/growth" initiatives	Low priority: ... ...
Reach peak performance		Very high priority:	Majority of "peak" initiatives

Next, decide how many quarters or years it will take you to execute this plan? Two years? Three years? Five years? Put in the years at the top.

Lastly, give each of your years a strategic theme. In my proposal from the "prioritization" chapter, I used the themes: "Laying the foundation for success" for the first year, "Great people for innovation and growth" for the second year, and "Reaching peak performance" for the third year. Maybe you like these themes, but it is often even better if you find strategic themes of your own. They need to be emotional, inspirational, and they need to reflect the DNA of your company.

This is it. Now you have a solid first draft of your personal game plan to take your company to full potential. The next step is to discuss this draft with your senior management team. Solicit their ideas, and ponder whether it is ambitious enough or too ambitious. Take enough time to have this discussion and ensure that there are no interruptions. Change the draft based on their input.

This step of soliciting ideas and creating buy-in is very important. Everybody around the table needs to feel that they have co-created the game plan. Everybody needs to buy into it. It will be hard work to execute the plan, so you need to make sure that everybody is on board. Everybody needs to feel that the plan will indeed drive your business to full potential. Everybody needs to feel that this is the right plan. You need to see excitement in everybody's eyes.

MOVING TO ACTION: QUESTIONS TO ASK YOURSELF

- ✓ What is the best way to have this discussion with your management team? When do you plan to have the discussion? Is this during an off-site meeting where you will not be interrupted?
- ✓ How do you operationalize the strategic initiatives (which quarterly deliverables/by when/who responsible/who do we need to involve/how do we measure success/how do we capture the benefits quickly)?
- ✓ How do you communicate the strategic themes to your employees ("why," passion/examples, inspirational, key action steps to achieve)?
- ✓ What are areas where you can realize quick wins to capture the momentum on these strategic initiatives?

51. Next Steps—Where to Take It from Here

> *"Do the difficult things while they are easy and do the great things while they are small. A journey of a thousand miles must begin with a single step."*
>
> — Lao Tzu

10x Results "Million $ Idea"

Take action. Take action now.

You do not have to have everything perfectly laid out. Take the first step. Enlist the support of your key people. Get them on board. Only when you take action can you achieve great things.

So, to make it more specific: **For your next management meeting, take the notes that you made in this book and put them up for discussion.**

Reserve four hours for this discussion. Start it off with just three questions:

(1) What is our vision of what our company should look like five years from now (toward customers, toward our employees, toward the community, financially)? Is it ambitious enough?

(2) Where are we falling short today?

> **(3) What do we have to do to close these gaps and 10x the results of our company over the next five years?**
>
> That is the first step. Take it, and you will be amazed at what comes after.

If you choose to, we can be your partner on this journey. Our firm, 10x Results Partners, works hand in hand with CEOs, business owners, and their management teams to create the exceptional results that you aspire to. Sometimes, it needs someone with an outside perspective to help your management team realize and believe that your company can be so much more than what you are currently aspiring to.

It is your choice. You are in the driver's seat. If you choose to partner with us, these are some of the benefits that you can expect:

The 10x Results Partners Principles

- ✓ **More results:** Together with you and your management team, we develop your personalized full potential plan. This full potential plan typically results in 2x, 5x, or even 10x the profits of what some of your management colleagues may have thought possible.
- ✓ **Much faster:** Results are being realized much faster than what was initially planned. We balance between quick, short-term results and addressing the more structural, long-term issues.
- ✓ **Sustainable:** By effectively prioritizing and freeing up your people's time from low-value activities, we ensure that your team does not burn out. Rather the opposite: They will feel more energized by seeing the positive results come in.
- ✓ **True partners:** We are confident that we can deliver what we promise. Therefore, we put a significant share of our profes-

sional fees at risk—contingent on your satisfaction with us. We are successful only when you are successful. That is what we call aligned incentives, and that is what we call true partnership.

There are three main ways of working with us:

THE 10X RESULTS PARTNERS PROGRAMS

- ✓ **10x Results Booster program:** This program is designed for small and medium-size businesses and entrepreneurs. This program consists of a series of web-based, in-depth workshops to help you develop your personal 10x Results full potential plan. It includes a detailed workbook with powerful checklists and templates. In video sessions, I will personally guide you step by step through the process of creating your own personal 10x Results full potential plan. This program runs once a quarter. Seats to this program typically sell out within hours. Through this program, you will get access to the 10x Results community of like-minded individuals. You can use this as the starting point for your personal mastermind group.
  You can find all details at www.10x-results.com/booster
- ✓ **10x Results Full Potential program:** In this program, I will personally work with you and your senior management team in your facilities to develop your full potential plan, and in the process, ensure full buy-in by all key stakeholders. If you wish, we will also accompany you all the way through implementation to full potential. Companies in this program typically have revenues of more than $1 billion. The minimum revenue threshold is $100 million.
  You can find all details at www.10x-results.com/fullpotential
- ✓ **10x Results Keynote:** The keynote speech is designed mainly

for company senior management team conferences and leading industry events. I will personally deliver a keynote speech of around 45 to 90 minutes to your group of Executives and Senior Managers. At the end of the keynote, everybody in the room (1) will walk out with a MUCH higher ambition level, (2) will understand that also in your company and in your industry 10x Results is possible, and (3) will be excited to start this journey right away.

You can find all details at www.10x-results.com/keynote

This brings this book to a close. I hope you found many new insights in this book. Insights that you can profitably leverage for your business to realize its full potential. Personally, I hope that you keep this book close to you. That you use it as your guide to take your company to full potential. That you read and reread it. That you discuss it with your management team. That you share it with your friends and close business associates.

On this, I actually have one request of you: If you found this book valuable and helpful, I ask you to share the insights and give this book as a gift to 10 of your closest friends and business colleagues who you want to succeed in life. Please also recommend this book to 20 other friends and business colleagues who you believe can significantly benefit from it. You may also want to give this book to your executives and managers at work so that you all speak the same language, follow the same principles, and jointly drive your business to full potential.

Ultimately, we are all in this world to make a difference—to have a positive impact on our families and the people around us. To build great companies with passionate employees who deliver great products and services to our customers. To have an impact in our communities and the world at large. I hope that this book can help you on this journey. I hope that this book will help you make your business the best that it can be—to realize 10x Results.

Acknowledgments

I am grateful to all clients who I worked with over the past two decades. I have learned a lot from working hand in hand with you and tackling some of your toughest problems. Every page in this book is inspired by the work that we have done together.

I am also grateful to all mentors who have helped me to become the person I am today. My parents, Anette and Bernd, who always supported me and had trust in my abilities. My teachers and professors at university and graduate school who taught me to look one level deeper and ask one more question. My mentors at work who have invested their personal time in my professional development.

Finally, I am most grateful to my family—my beloved wife, Asiel, who encouraged me to write this book, and our children, Laura and Albert, who give our life deep meaning and purpose.

About the Author

Marc Will is a Senior Partner & Director at 10x Results Partners. He helps ambitious business owners and CEOs bring their companies to full potential. He is an expert in driving profitable growth, improving company performance, multiplying employee productivity and engagement, and setting companies up for long-term success.

Over the past two decades, Marc supported many clients, ranging from large multinationals to entrepreneur-run businesses and internet startups. His past clients come from more than 30 different industries, including industrial goods and services, high tech, transportation, telecommunications, retail, and financial services.

Marc was a Board member for Europe at one of the top 100 companies in the world (Fortune Global 100). He was responsible for the transformation efforts (business processes, digitalization, IT) in one of the company's divisions. In addition, he was also responsible for strategy, BPO, and customer service.

For 10+ years, Marc worked at one of the world's leading strategy consulting firms. He holds an MBA from Thunderbird, the world's premier business school in international management. He lives with his wife and their two children in Munich.

Printed in Great Britain
by Amazon